STOP
FOLLOWING THE
RULES

THE REAL-WORLD GUIDE TO
BUILDING FINANCIAL SECURITY

RYAN M. COULTER, CFP®

Published by InnoGage Publishing
Warrenton, Virginia
www.innogagency.com/publishing
InnoGage Publishing is a registered trademark of InnoGage Holdings, LLC.

ISBN: 979-8-9942309-0-9 Hardcover
ISBN: 979-8-9942309-1-6 Paperback
ISBN: 979-8-9942309-2-3 Ebook
LCCN: 2026901172

Printed in the United States of America.

This publication is designed to provide accurate and authoritative information with regard to the subject matter covered. It is sold with the understanding that neither the author nor the publisher is engaged in rendering legal, accounting, or other professional services. If expert assistance is required, the services of a competent professional should be sought.

Publisher's Mission: *InnoGage Publishing* is passionate about empowering authors to share their unique voices and bring impactful ideas to life. We specialize in transforming concepts into beautifully crafted books that inspire, captivate, and resonate with readers around the globe. If you're ready to turn your manuscript or book idea into something extraordinary, we'd love to hear from you.

Visit us at www.innogagency.com/contact-us to get started.

TABLE OF CONTENTS

FOREWORD

There's a moment in every professional's life when they realize that simply following the rules doesn't lead to the results they hoped for. I remember the first time I met Ryan Coulter years ago, when he was already beginning to question those rules. He was thoughtful, smart, and unwilling to accept that "standard" financial advice was truly helping families achieve lasting security.

From the start, Ryan stood out. He had that rare combination of technical skill and genuine empathy that can't be taught. Ryan listened more than he spoke. And when he did speak, he had a way of turning the financial jargon that confuses so many people into simple, logical concepts that made sense. It was clear early on that he was a top advisor.

HOW I KNOW RYAN—AND WHY HIS PERSPECTIVE MATTERS

Over the years, I've had the privilege of working closely with Ryan through Lifetime Financial Growth, where we share a mission of helping individuals and families build balance and confidence in their financial lives. I've watched him evolve from a top advisor into one of the most respected professionals in our field. He's not content with mediocrity, instead he challenges assumptions—starting with his own—and searches for what truly works in the real world.

That pursuit of truth is what makes Ryan so effective. He doesn't approach planning as a formula to be followed, but as a process of discovery. He helps people see how money actually moves through their lives, how protection and opportunity coexist, and how financial security is built by design.

Ryan's credibility comes from years of hands-on experience—working with high-income earners, business owners, healthcare professionals, and families across the country. He's built his practice around education and empowerment, not sales and slogans. And that's exactly what you'll experience in the pages ahead.

WHY THIS BOOK IS DIFFERENT

The financial world is saturated with advice—often contradictory, frequently confusing, and almost always oversimplified. "Save more. Spend less. Max out your 401(k). Pay off your mortgage early." We've all heard these rules of thumb, and at first glance, they sound reasonable. But when applied blindly, they can lead to a lifetime of uncertainty and missed opportunity.

Ryan's message in *Stop Following the Rules* is both refreshing and necessary: the conventional playbook doesn't work for everyone. Real financial confidence comes not from copying someone else's formula, but from understanding your own. This book invites you to think differently—to question what you've been told, to challenge old assumptions, and to create a plan that fits your actual life, not just a spreadsheet.

What I love most about Ryan's writing is that it's not abstract or theoretical. Every principle in this book is grounded in the realities of his daily work with clients. These ideas have been tested, refined, and proven in the real world. Whether he's explaining how to maximize cash flow, rethink debt, or protect your income and assets, Ryan never loses sight of the ultimate goal: peace of mind.

A MODERN APPROACH TO AN AGE-OLD PROBLEM

At its core, financial planning is about trade-offs—balancing today's priorities with tomorrow's possibilities. But most people have been taught to view money through a narrow lens. They see saving and investing as separate from living, protection as separate from growth, and planning as something you do "later."

Ryan bridges those gaps beautifully. He shows how protection, liquidity, and growth are interconnected and part of a cohesive strategy. He explains how true wealth isn't about chasing returns; it's about creating stability, flexibility, and freedom. And he does it with a rare authenticity that makes complex ideas feel approachable.

THE MAN BEHIND THE MESSAGE

Ryan's background shaped his unique approach. A graduate of Penn State with a degree in kinesiology, he's always had an instinct for how systems work—the human body, the mind, and the financial world. He understands that strength and endurance, whether physical or financial, come from balance and consistency, not extremes.

That perspective informs every conversation he has with clients and every insight he shares in this book. He's built his career by focusing not on products, but on people. Not on transactions, but on trust. That's why clients don't just work with Ryan once; they stay with him for years, often for life.

When you read his words, you'll sense his integrity. He's direct, but never condescending. Analytical, but never rigid. And most of all, deeply human.

WHY YOU SHOULD KEEP READING

If you've ever wondered why doing "all the right things" still leaves you feeling uncertain about your financial future, this book is for you. It's for anyone who's tired of guessing, tired of feeling behind, or tired of wondering if you're missing something. Ryan will give you a new lens—a way to see your finances not as a collection of accounts and statements, but as a dynamic, living system that supports your goals and values.

By the time you finish *Stop Following the Rules*, you'll understand why traditional advice so often falls short and what to do instead. You'll have a clearer sense of how to protect what matters most, create sustainable income, and make confident decisions for yourself and your family.

MY ENCOURAGEMENT AND MY CHALLENGE TO YOU

As someone who has spent decades mentoring advisors and helping families across the country, I can say with certainty: this book is the **real deal**. Ryan's approach is balanced, evidence based, and rooted in genuine care for the people he serves. He's not trying to impress you, he's trying to equip you.

So here's my challenge to you as a reader: don't just skim these pages—engage with them. Let them challenge your assumptions and sharpen your perspective. Use them as a guide to build clarity, confidence, and control in your financial life.

I'm proud to call Ryan a colleague and a friend. His voice is one of reason in an industry that often confuses motion with progress. In a time when so many people are searching for direction, this book provides it with honesty, precision, and heart.

Enjoy what follows. And as Ryan reminds us, sometimes the best way to move forward is to **stop following the rules**.

David Hausdorff,

Executive Vice President, Lifetime Financial Growth

INTRODUCTION

Money touches every part of our lives, yet most of us were never taught how to think about it with clarity or confidence. We learn bits and pieces along the way—from parents, friends, colleagues, or articles we skim online—but rarely do we find a framework that helps us put it all together. Too often financial planning is presented as a collection of rules, products, or quick fixes rather than as a process for building the kind of life we actually want.

When I first started working with clients, I thought my role was to provide answers. Over time I discovered that my greatest responsibility was to help people ask the right questions. What do you really want your money to do for you? What does financial security look like for your family? How do you make decisions today that will give you freedom, not regret, tomorrow?

This book is the result of those conversations. It reflects years of listening to people from all walks of life (business owners, healthcare professionals, engineers, technology leaders, and families) share their hopes, frustrations, and fears about money. It also presents my conviction that the best financial strategies are not about chasing returns or buying products but about building confidence.

Inside you will not find magic formulas or one-size-fits-all prescriptions. Instead, you will find principles and practices that can help you make informed decisions, avoid costly mistakes, and move toward the future with greater confidence. Whether you are just getting started, planning for retirement, or somewhere in between, my hope is that this book gives you tools to think differently about money and to act with purpose.

Ultimately, financial planning is not about numbers on a page. It is about aligning your resources with your values so that you can live fully today while preparing wisely for tomorrow. If this book helps you take even one step closer to that goal, then it will have done its job.

CHAPTER 1

MAKING SENSE OF YOUR FINANCES

B artering, buying, banking. If there's one thing about human society that separates us from the rest of creation, it's that we've created a system that represents hours worked, products made, and perceived value. You learn it when you lose a tooth as a child and find a crisp dollar bill under your pillow in its place.

With such a universal truth uniting us all, you would think the average person is probably good with money. Advice swarms the internet and barrages our televisions: buy now, sell now, invest now, save now, 401(k)s, retirement, inflation. You can't escape it.

And yet—

We all know at least two things about finances:

1. You need to be able to make and manage money to survive.
2. Eventually you will have to pay taxes.

However, much like the rest of the world, the jobs, earning methods, and ways we save money have evolved significantly over the past twenty years. But the types of people who offer financial advice online and on television shows haven't realized it yet. And therefore their audiences are suffering. Because if the kinds of financial advice that people give out worked, then why are people still struggling and living paycheck to paycheck, drowning in debt?

A conversation I had with my father illustrates the growing divide between the finances of the past and those of the future. My claim was: It's basically impossible to live on $50,000 a year as a college graduate in the modern world. He looked at me like I'd just told him the NFL was going bankrupt.

Sure, in 1987 that salary could buy you a house, a sedan, and an aboveground pool. But today? That's just enough to rent a studio apartment, finance a car you can't afford, and keep your student loan interest rate mildly in check.

Imagine the modern family of today. They've got one child already in daycare, and both parents work full-time jobs just to make ends meet. Now, all of a sudden, they've got a second child on the way. Their financial needs just doubled in size. They now need two cars if they don't already have them. They need a new house to meet the needs of their growing family. And they'll require a pretty hefty surplus to pay for the additional child's daycare, healthcare needs, food, clothes, and all the other supplies to keep a child happy and healthy.

But wait, there's more!

Roughly fifty percent of the American population has some sort of postsecondary education they must pay for, usually out of pocket.[1] Most decent professions require some sort of education or certification just to get your foot in the door. You need to have a degree to survive, unless you're looking into building houses or flipping burgers. And even then, chefs and builders will be the first to tell you that anyone in their profession still needs to learn skills to get ahead. You literally can't afford not to invest in your education. So, on top of your family's bills, you and probably your spouse are likely making payments on your student loans.

Then there's the car. You need it to get to work, because teleportation still hasn't made it out of beta testing. That's another $600 a month. Toss in rent (a modest $1,755, if you enjoy natural lighting and walls),[2] and you're already $3,000 deep before you've even bought a single can of beans or a bag of dry rice.

If you're like most people, you do the math, panic slightly, and check your bank account. Still empty. And here's the unbelievable part: *you did everything right.*

You followed the advice. You went to school. You got the job. You didn't buy a Tesla or a Mercedes. And still, you're barely staying afloat. The experts on Reddit and Instagram tell you to "just stop buying lattes," as if Starbucks and avocado toast were holding your wallet hostage. Some will even suggest you

---

[1] Michael T. Nietzel, "Percentage of U.S. Adults with College Degrees Edges Higher, Finds Lumina Report," *Forbes*, February 1, 2024, accessed July 23, 2025, https://www.forbes.com/sites/michaeltnietzel/2024/02/01/percentage-of-us-adults-with-college-degrees-edges-higher-finds-lumina-report/.

[2] "Average Rent in the U.S. & Rent Prices by State," *RentCafe*, last updated June 2025, accessed July 23, 2025, https://www.rentcafe.com/average-rent-market-trends/us/

move to a cheaper state, which sounds great, until you realize your family, your job, and your childcare are all inconveniently located *here*.

You're not dumb. You're not lazy. You're just navigating a system that's increasingly indifferent to how hard you're trying. That means it's time to work smarter, not harder, and figure out how to manage your money without losing your mind.

This book isn't here to shame you, sell you a magic budget spreadsheet, or lecture you on the evils of buying yourself a little treat one Friday when you're stuck in traffic. It's here to talk about *what actually works* for real people, living real lives, trying to make actual progress in a world where $100 of groceries now buys you three lemons and a box of cereal.

Because the truth is, the system isn't broken. It's working exactly the way it was designed to. It's the advice that is broken and it isn't really advice at all. It's the sales pitches disguised as advice in dark corners, waiting for you to buy a product instead of truly addressing the issues with your spending habits. Mainstream financial gurus want to make money off you instead of helping you find out how to improve your life.

The real question is: *what are you going to do about it?*

MAKING SENSE OF A MESS

You're an adult with responsibilities, hopes, and dreams. You've decided to take control of your money. You start searching for financial advice online from people who might know what they are talking about. Five minutes later, you're either in a full-blown existential crisis or halfway through a YouTube video promising to retire you by forty-two if you just open the *right* kind of IRA and stop ordering Uber Eats.

Here's the problem with this approach: everyone's an expert, and none of them agree.

One article tells you to max out your 401(k). The very next one says, "Don't touch your 401(k), do a Roth IRA instead." Neither explains what either one actually does. But both are delivered with absolute certainty, and possibly a stock photo of a suspiciously cheerful couple holding coffee mugs and gazing at their ambiguous future, probably in a home they can't afford.

But neither of these statements is a real financial plan. These are just products. Retirement plans, accounts, and conversion strategies are like toolboxes. They might have everything you need, but they come with no instructions on how to get your desired result. No one ever tells you what you're building. And without a plan, all those tools might as well be an IKEA parts foreign language instruction manual: technically useful, but practically useless (unless you speak fluent Swedish).

But let's not let the professionals off the hook here. Too many financial advisors aren't much better. They cling to the same advice they've been parroting since the fax machine was state-of-the-art: *Max out your retirement plan at work.* No context. No real strategy. Just vibes.

Then suddenly—plot twist—they're telling you to do a Roth IRA conversion. Why? "It's good for taxes." Okay ... but *your* taxes? This year? In retirement?

No one explains *why* the move makes sense. But without a strategy, without any sense of timing, goals, trade-offs, or co-ordination, you're just jumping from one shiny idea to the next and calling it a plan. So let's pause here and clear up a few things.

FIVE COMMON FINANCIAL MISCONCEPTIONS THAT MAKE SMART PEOPLE FEEL STUPID

► **"If I just max out my 401(k), I'm set for retirement."** You might be "set" for retirement the same way buying protein powder makes you a bodybuilder. Contributions aren't a strategy. They're just an activity. If you don't have liquid capital but have all your money tied up in your retirement accounts, you aren't doing it right.

► **"Roth IRAs are better than traditional IRAs."** That depends on your tax bracket now, your tax bracket later, your income limits, your investment timeline, and whether or not you enjoy reading IRS fine print in your free time. Since everyone has a different life and a different situation, it's important to consult with a licensed financial advisor to make sure you're making the right decision. Don't rely on some talking parrot on TV to help you.

► **"Budgeting will fix my financial problems."** Budgeting is painful, and it won't make housing cheaper or eggs cost less. If you're spending $5,000 a month and making $4,500, no spreadsheet will save you. If you're constantly changing your budget, the lack of consistency will cause bigger problems. And stop paying $8 a month for the budgeting app that you aren't using.

► **"Debt is always bad."** No. High interest debt that's funding your Amazon habit? Bad. A low interest mortgage that keeps a roof over your head while your money works for you elsewhere? That's called *leverage*. Credit card debt that's out of control is bad, but some credit card debt is acceptable, even recommended, because you need to have and build credit over time anyway.

► **"I should move to a cheaper state."** Sure. Leave your job, support system, and daycare options behind. But hey, the milk is twenty cents cheaper, and the housing market is *only* insane instead of apocalyptic. The problem with fleeing from inflation is that eventually it will catch up to you, whether this year or in five years.

Here's the point: it's not that this advice is *wrong*, it's that it's disconnected from your actual life. These are generic tactics pretending to be personalized strategies. And the difference matters.

What you really need isn't more "best practices." You need a framework. A strategy that fits *your* income, debt, goals, family, timeline, and stress level. The sooner you realize you're not crazy, and the system isn't really designed to be clear, the sooner you can start making smart decisions that actually fit *you*.

A BASIC MAP FOR EVERY FINANCIAL PLAN

We don't live in a spreadsheet. We live in the real world, where interest rates spike, cars break down, and your kid decides to audition for every extracurricular activity that involves expensive gear. Real financial planning starts with real life. So let's flip the script.

Here's the philosophy I use with my own clients. It's not flashy. It's not product-based. It doesn't involve chasing tax loopholes or playing stock market roulette. It's just—logical. There is no one-size-fits-all when it comes to financial planning. That's why you need a financial advisor to help you figure out the next steps.

But even the best financial planning can't start from scratch without any information. You're letting someone observe your personal life. You will have to offer some context for what they're seeing and inform them of your goals and weaknesses.

STEP ONE
Get Organized (No, Really. Find Your Stuff)

Before you can plan your finances, you need to know where they are. What do you own? What do you owe? Where are the accounts, the debts, the insurance policies, the forgotten 401(k)s from jobs you barely remember?

Yes, it's not ideal. But neither is getting caught without a password to your own retirement plan. No financial planner worth their salt will allow you to create a financial plan without these items.

Start by gathering the financial puzzle pieces; then we can actually begin solving the puzzle. It can be a paper copy, a folder, or as simple as an email with multiple attachments. But if you don't know, then we don't know.

STEP TWO
Protect Yourself (Because Life Happens, and It's Usually Expensive)

Here's a wild idea: plan for the bad stuff *before* it happens. Everyone wants to talk about investing and wealth, but nobody wants to talk about what happens when life punches you in the teeth. And life? It's got a hell of a right hook. If you have a family or own a home, you're open to several different catastrophes. Sit down with your loved ones and go over the worst-case scenarios together, so that you can figure out what you need and when you need it. This doesn't mean the worst will happen, but it will take away the anxiety of thinking that you aren't prepared.

You need a safety net. Insurance, emergency funds, legal documents—things that help keep your family safe, your assets protected, and your future intact if something goes sideways. Because guess what? At some point, something will go wrong. And when it does, your shiny Roth IRA won't help if you're draining it to pay for a medical emergency or legal fees. That is not liquid capital, and it won't give you the money you need to pay for surgery, time off from work, or home renovations.

STEP THREE
Create Cash Flow (No, Budgeting Alone isn't Enough)

You can't save what you don't have. So let's talk about cash flow—the beating heart of your financial life. This is where we reduce debt, lower taxes, and create breathing room. Not so you can feel smug over your mint-colored budgeting app, but so you can actually *live* and make progress.

Most people are told to start investing first. But investing when you're drowning in high interest debt or living paycheck to paycheck is like setting fire to your money with a very polite lighter. If you take half your paycheck and put it where you can't touch it, and then your kid comes home with a broken arm and you have to take off work, then what are you going to do? You're going to lean on loans and credit cards, which set you back. Create cash flow *first*, and everything else becomes doable.

STEP FOUR
Save Strategically (Not Just Automatically)

Once you've got protection and cash flow in place, then—and only then—do we talk about saving. But not just dumping money into the nearest retirement account because your HR rep said it was "smart."

You should have some concept of what you want to save for. If you find it too difficult to narrow it down specifically, then a meeting between you and a financial planner can help. We look at what you're saving for:

- ► Emergency fund?
- ► First home?
- ► Education for your kids?
- ► A real retirement that doesn't involve part-time dog walking?

You don't have to have a different account for every goal. You only need to save, invest, and then spend the rest on your life. It's crucial to make sure any savings accounts are also accessible to you when you need that money, not when the organization deems it necessary to give it to you. It's your money. You don't want to lose it.

STEP FIVE
Invest (Now You've Earned It)

Finally, we invest. Not because it's trendy. Not because your cousin got rich off crypto. But because you've built the foundation that makes investing powerful and sustainable.

This is where your money starts to work harder than you do. But it only works if the structure beneath it holds. You don't need to be a Warren Buffett or a Reddit investing genius to make it work for you. You just need a financial planner who knows what they are doing and who understands your needs and goals.

You also don't need to constantly change up your investments. Nine times out of ten, it's already too late to jump on a stock that's rapidly rising, because if *you're* hearing about it, then so is everyone else.

NO NEED TO PANIC

Money is a problem for every single person on the planet, rich and poor. Let's get one thing out of the way: you're not stupid, lazy, or irresponsible if you don't have your financial life perfectly sorted out. You're normal. And if you've ever sat through a financial webinar, tried to decode an "expert" blog post, or walked into a bank only to feel like a child asking how checking works, you're definitely not alone.

The real problem isn't that you've done something wrong. It's that the entire system is quietly rigged to make you feel like you have. Financial planning doesn't have to feel like punishment for the life you've lived so far. You don't need to be rich to get started. You don't need to feel guilty about that time you maxed out a credit card buying plane tickets to a wedding you didn't even enjoy.

Most generic financial advice starts with *what* to buy.
"Open a Roth IRA!"
"Get a life insurance policy!"
"Invest in index funds!"
"Buy gold and live off the grid!"

That's not a plan. That's a grocery list written by strangers.

Here's the truth: if you have the *right* plan in place, one based on your life, your income, your risks, and your priorities, then the *products* take care of themselves. The right decisions become obvious. And they're often simpler than you've been led to believe.

Planning is what gives you confidence. Products are just tools. And a good financial planner makes sure you're not being sold a hammer when what you really need is a flashlight.

People often get lost in the details, trying to make sure bad things don't happen to them. But that's similar to making sure that you won't ever get sick. Everyone gets sick. Markets fluctuate. Taxes change. Inflation shows up uninvited. You can't predict the future, but you *can* prepare for it.

There are only two things that really matter in financial planning:

1. **BEING PROTECTED** when things go sideways.
2. **SAVING ENOUGH** when things are going well.

That's it. That's the list.

If you're protected and you're saving, you're ahead of ninety percent of the population. And once those two are in place, the rest (investments, retirement strategies, college funds, vacation homes in the Bahamas) start to fall in line. The goal here isn't perfection. It's *progress*. And confidence. Once you stop tying your self-worth to your net worth, financial planning becomes a lot less terrifying and a lot more effective.

THE TEN COMMANDMENTS OF REAL FINANCIAL PLANNING

*(Because "Thou Shalt Not Panic" isn't
printed on enough bank statements)*

1. **Thou Shalt Not Mistake a Product for Strategy.** Maxing out your 401(k) without knowing why does not make you a financial genius. It makes you someone with a tax-deferred mystery account and no idea what retirement actually looks like.

2. **Thou Shalt Not Worship Financial Products.** Roth IRA, Traditional IRA, 401(k), SEP, and HSA are not your plan. They're just containers. Don't confuse the toolbox with the blueprint. Many people have all of these products and no plan.

3. **Thou Shalt Get Organized Before Getting Advice.**
    If you don't know what you have, what you owe, or where it's all hiding, then no advisor, algorithm, or app is going to save you. Start by cleaning up your financial junk drawer. The sooner you get to it, the less work you'll have to do.

4. **Thou Shalt Protect Thyself First.** Before you invest a dime, ensure your ability to earn it. You can't build wealth while bailing water from a leaky financial boat.

5. **Thou Shalt Create Cash Flow Before Chasing Gains.** If you're living paycheck to paycheck, "diversifying your portfolio" is just a fancy way of saying "I hope this works out." How is that different from gambling your paycheck away?

6. **Thou Shalt Not Be Ashamed of Thy Balance Sheet.** Debt doesn't make you a failure. A small income doesn't mean you're not trying. Shame is not a financial plan— clarity is. You can live a fantastic life while making an average salary. It's all about the details.

7. **Thou Shalt Plan Before Paying Off Everything.** Paying down debt feels good, but wiping out all your cash to do it? That's just giving your future emergencies a head start. You know what that leads to? More debt, and less progress.

8. **Thou Shalt Focus on What You Can Control.** You can't predict the market. You can't guess your future tax rate. But you can save, protect, and prepare like a person who reads footnotes.

9. **Thou Shalt Not DIY Thy Financial Life Without a Real Map.** Google is not a plan. ChatGPT is not your advisor. And your cousin who once sold insurance probably isn't your financial guru. You need a financial planner who is certified, knowledgeable, tested, and listens to you.

10. **Thou Shalt Remember: A Small Plan Beats a Big Guess.** It's better to have a modest income and a solid plan than six figures and six panic attacks a year. More money doesn't solve a lack of strategy. Planning does.

YOU NEED TO START FINANCIAL PLANNING NOW!

There's a great lie buried in modern life, and it goes something like this:

"I'll start saving when things calm down."

Spoiler: Things don't calm down. Ever. If you have a family, a life, a hobby, a house, a car, you'll always be facing some crisis. Even if you don't have any of those things, you'll still run into some sort of problem that requires money to fix. There will always be a tire that needs replacing, a wedding that needs a gift, a water heater that waits patiently until 2:00 a.m. on a holiday weekend to burst. That's life. It's chaotic. It's expensive. And it doesn't come with an intermission.

So let's be clear: the best time to start financial planning was yesterday. The second-best time is right now. The longer you wait to plan, the fewer options you have. Compound interest? Works best when it has decades to do its thing. Protection strategies like life insurance or disability coverage? Only affordable and easy to get when you're young and healthy, which, I hate to break it to you, you are never going to be more of than you are *today*.

If your master plan is to "wait until things settle," you may be unknowingly settling into something worse: a life where financial stress is permanent background noise. That kind of life has no quality at all. Most financial advice assumes you'll stay healthy, stable, and employed until you ride off into a well funded sunset. But what happens when you don't?

A key to financial survival lies in having insurance, or protection, for your assets. However, insurance premiums are based on two things:

1. Your age
2. Your health

Spoiler: neither of those is trending in your favor. You're only getting older, and your health is only going to become more fragile over time. Every year you delay protection, it almost certainly gets more expensive, or worse, unavailable. That policy you shrugged off at thirty-five might be ten times the cost (or completely out of reach) at sixty. And trust me: no one wants to be sixty-five, newly retired, and suddenly told by Uncle Sam that their estate plan is a flaming bag of taxes.

Can you start planning at fifty-five? Sure. But it's not the same game anymore. At thirty-five, you've got thirty years of compounding ahead of you. At fifty-five, you've got maybe ten. That's not a moral failure, it's just math. And math, as it turns out, does not care how good your intentions were.

Even if you're "late," there's still plenty of good to be done: reducing taxes, paying off debt smartly, and building a cushion that brings peace of mind. But let's not kid ourselves, the earlier you start, the more options you have. And the more mistakes you can afford to make.

DON'T LET DEBT GET YOU DOWN

There is no rate of return on earth that will outpace a twenty-one percent credit card interest rate. That kind of debt is financial quicksand, and millions of people are silently sinking in it. Not because they're lazy. Not because they're bad with money. But because *life happened faster than their paychecks could catch up.*

If you're in debt and stressed, welcome to the club. You're not broken. You're just overdue for a better plan. Traditional advice suggests that you should allocate every extra dollar towards paying off your debt until it's completely gone. Logical? Sure. Helpful? Not really. Here's the problem: life doesn't stop while you pay down your balances. If you spend all your spare cash hammering away at your loans and credit cards and *don't* have a backup plan, guess what happens when life hits you with a $1,200 car repair?

You're right back in debt. Again. That's why the avalanche/ snowball method sounds great in theory but often backfires in practice. You pay aggressively. Life punches back. You drain your savings. And the cycle starts all over.

And no, you can't just run away from credit cards and credit scores. Modern life almost demands that we have at least one credit card. Emergencies can sometimes be solved with a credit card. So religiously avoiding credit cards doesn't make sense. What if we tried something smarter?

EMERGENCY FUNDS > EXTRA PAYMENTS

Let's say your minimum student loan payment is $500/month. You're paying $700, thinking you're winning the debt game. But if you don't have emergency savings, that extra $200 is *better off in the bank*. Because when—not if—life comes calling, it's your savings that let you *stay out* of debt.

Forget the six-months-of-expenses rule. That's outdated. What you actually need, in most cases, is around $20,000 in accessible cash. Why $20K? Because if you've got your protection dialed in (health, disability, life, home, auto, umbrella), there's almost *nothing* in modern life that can hit you with a bigger bill than that. And in my quest to avoid generic truths, I'll even admit that some of you might need more than that, and some of you might need less. But on average, $20K covers that first hospital payment, a few months of living without employment, car repairs, or a hotel stay because your basement flooded. If you need more money than that, we're going to have a different conversation about your situation. Something might need to change. But that's another book.

FINANCIAL STRESS STARTS EARLY

Most people experience financial stress starting in college. You're nineteen, juggling textbooks, two part-time jobs, and ramen that tastes like anxiety. Your parents either hand you cash without context or throw you into the world with a "Good luck!" and a Costco card.

Did you learn about managing money in high school?

Probably not. Did your parents explain any of it to you? Probably not. Did your grandfather's financial cliches repeated *ad nauseam* get through to you? No, and it was outdated and poorly explained. There might be a few exceptions to these situations (maybe your father was a respected financial advisor), but in general, we've been taught that we're on our own when it comes to money.

No one teaches you how to deal with debt. No one teaches you how to protect yourself. And absolutely no one teaches you how to *not feel ashamed* when money gets tight. But here's the thing: that shame? It's optional. You don't need to suffer your way to financial health. You just need a framework and a little grace.

Let's reframe this in millennial terms: building an emergency fund is self-care. Automating your savings is emotional regulation. Protecting your income is the grown-up version of drinking water and stretching before bed.

Here's what *actually works*:

► **AUTOMATE YOUR SAVINGS.** Don't wait to save "what's left." There will never be anything left. Set up fifteen–twenty percent of your *gross income* to save before you see it.

► **BUILD YOUR EMERGENCY FUND.** Aim for $20,000 in cash. Not investments. Not retirement accounts—*Cash*. Because real emergencies don't care about early withdrawal penalties. It should take you less than an hour to access what's in your emergency fund. It's for emergencies.

► **MAXIMIZE YOUR PROTECTION.** Health, disability, life, auto, umbrella, and legal documents must be done early. Group insurance at work is a start, but not a solution. Figure out your vulnerabilities and shield up before they become serious problems.

► **STOP GLORIFYING SIDE HUSTLES.** If your main hustle can't support your life, the answer isn't Uber Eats at 10:00 p.m. It's a new job. More income, better benefits, more peace. You cannot max out your working hours running around hoping to collect more cash. You'll run out of gas very quickly. Then you'll be burned out with no hope of getting back on track.

► **GET PROFESSIONAL HELP.** Your cousin's financial advisor is not *your* advisor. Taking secondhand advice from someone who doesn't know your goals, income, or emotional triggers is like borrowing someone else's prescription glasses: blurry, disorienting, and not great for your long-term vision.

IF YOU'RE ALREADY OVERWHELMED, YOU'RE NOT ALONE

Maybe you've been procrastinating. Perhaps you're worried about what the numbers will reveal. Maybe you're worried that financial planning will mean you have to live like a monk for the next fifteen years.

Here's the truth: *Good financial planning makes you comfortable.* It *reduces* your stress. It provides you a sense of confidence. It gives you the freedom to enjoy your money, *because you know the essentials are already covered.* If you're drowning in debt, the solution isn't to hustle harder. It's time to step back, organize, and design a system that actually *works with your life.* Because money is only stressful when it's unpredictable. Once you've got a plan, you might actually experience five minutes of peace, which is worth more than any finance guru's advice.

CHAPTER 2

DOES FINANCIAL PLANNING ACTUALLY WORK?

I f you still aren't convinced about the applicability of financial gurus' advice, guess what? Financial planning, as most people know it, doesn't work. If it did, most Americans wouldn't be one flat tire away from a full-blown financial crisis.

Think about it. Most of us followed the advice. We got a good degree. We got the office job. We signed up for a 401(k) plan. We made the "aggressive" decision to throw every spare dollar at our student loans. And still, nearly sixty percent of Americans couldn't cover a $1,000 emergency without going into debt or raiding their retirement accounts.[3] That's not because

---

3   Anne Marie D. Lee, "Most Americans Can't Afford a $1,000 Emergency Expense, Report Finds," *CBS News* (MoneyWatch), updated January 23, 2025, accessed July 24, 2025, https://www.cbsnews.com/news/saving-money-emergency-expenses-2025/

people aren't trying, saving, or planning. The current advice is outdated, out of touch, and often completely backwards.

Finance celebrities and personalities only seem to know three things when it comes to money:

1. Get out of debt.
2. Max out your retirement plan.
3. Budget better.

It sounds good until life happens. You get sick. You lose your job. Your car needs $1,400 worth of repairs, and the same week, your kid needs a dental procedure that isn't covered by insurance. If you cut any more costs, you won't be able to afford extracurricular activities for your child or even a simple road trip over the weekend. Suddenly, your carefully followed plan collapses, and the only way out is to generate more income, whether from a second job or a business venture that unexpectedly succeeds.

The real problem isn't that you're not doing enough. The problem is that the financial system you were taught to trust is built for a world that does not exist. So why do people still believe this system works? Because it looks like it should. It's neat. It's logical. It sounds responsible. You're told that investing early and getting out of debt make you a grown-up. And, sure, on paper, in a spreadsheet, in theory, everything checks out.

But in the real world? That rigid advice becomes fragile. One emergency, layoff, or medical bill can wipe out months or years of hard work and progress. It's time to rethink the plan. Not because you failed at financial planning, but because financial planning failed you. If you're still living paycheck to paycheck even with a good job, then the general "budget harder" advice may not apply.

As initially intended, financial planning was meant to bring a personalized approach to each individual's financial goals and desires. The general cliches of saving more, making more, and spending less sound great, but they don't help you manage emergencies, messy life moments, or expensive dreams you want to check off your list.

THE REALITY OF RETIREMENT

For decades, financial advisors, workplace HR packets, and retirement commercials have all sung the same song: If you just contribute to your retirement plan and maybe throw in a Roth IRA for flair, you'll be just fine. But if that's true, why are more than seventeen million Americans age sixty-five+ economically insecure?[4] Why are so many people relying almost entirely on Social Security to get by? Why are we still telling people that being a "401(k) millionaire" is the dream, when in reality that money may be the only thing standing between them and going broke in retirement? There's an apparent disconnect between what we're told and what happens.

One of the most repeated myths in financial planning is that you'll need "less income" in retirement, usually around seventy percent of what you made while working.[5] Why? Supposedly,

---

[4] National Council on Aging (NCOA), "Get the Facts on Economic Security for Seniors," *National Council on Aging*, June 1, 2024, accessed July 24, 2025, https://www.ncoa.org/article/get-the-facts-on-economic-security-for-seniors/.

[5] Experian, "What Is the 70% Rule for Retirement Savings?" *Ask Experian* (blog), published approximately 1.8 years ago (ca. January 2024), accessed July 24, 2025, https://www.experian.com/blogs/ask-experian/what-is-70-percent-rule-for-retirement-savings/.

you'll be in a lower tax bracket, your mortgage will be paid off, and your lifestyle will magically shrink into a smaller, more affordable version of itself. Let's test that logic.

What days do most people spend the most money? Saturday and Sunday. Why? Because they're off. And when people have time, they live their lives. They shop. They eat out. They travel. They spend. Retirement is seven Saturdays in a row. Now ask yourself: Will you want *less* income when you finally have time to enjoy life? Will you be content clipping coupons and skipping visits to your grandkids so you can "stay within your four percent withdrawal rate"? Because that's what traditional advice says: take four percent from your nest egg each year, and try not to touch the principal. Never mind that you've worked your entire adult life to build this pile of money. Now you're supposed to look at it and say, "*No thanks. I'll just take the crumbs off the top.*"

Another lie baked into the "you'll need less income" story is that your expenses will drop. Spoiler: they won't, especially not the one that matters most, healthcare. Healthcare costs don't go down with age. They go up. So do medication costs. So do supplemental insurance premiums. And no, Medicare doesn't cover everything. Even if you've got a decent retirement account, one medical emergency can send your entire plan into a tailspin, especially if you haven't planned for elder care or major out-of-pocket expenses.

Another thing that won't stop is Inflation. Inflation doesn't stop as soon as you stop working. Cost for groceries, travel, utilities, and insurance all continue to climb. And if your plan is built on the idea that you'll be "in a lower bracket," but you've done a good job saving and investing—congratulations, you're actually in a *higher* one.

If you've ever been told that you'll need less income in retirement or that you'll be in a lower tax bracket, please delete that advice from your brain. That idea only works if your retirement plan involves sitting quietly in a dark room eating saltines. But if you want to travel, visit family, donate to causes you care about, or enjoy your life, then you're going to need just as much income (or more). And here's the twist: if you're successful, if you've saved well, invested smart, and done all the right things, you might actually end up in a *higher* tax bracket in retirement, which makes tax strategy, not just savings rate, critical.

Next the idea of becoming a 401(k) millionaire gets tossed around like it's some kind of golden ticket. But let's do some math. Pretend you've got a million dollars in your retirement account. That's a big deal. But if you're following the conservative withdrawal advice of four percent, you're taking out *$40,000 per year*. After taxes, maybe $32,000. Try living on that. You're looking at a lifestyle that runs on ramen noodles and living in someone's basement, or even worse, a van down by the river. And here's the punchline: if you're in a place where you *have to* withdraw more, because Social Security isn't enough and inflation is outpacing your budget, you'll eat into your principal and your money will start shrinking faster than it can grow.

You worked for forty years and now you have to ask permission—from your spreadsheet—to take a vacation? Your retirement plan can't just be "accumulate, then cross your fingers." It needs to be structured around *cash flow, protection,* and *liquidity.* You need:

► Liquid savings for emergencies
► Insurance to guard against the unexpected
► A strategy that lets you use your money, not just admire it from a distance

And yes, you need to enjoy your life, not just stretch your money until it snaps. Because the whole point of financial planning isn't to retire *responsibly*, it's to retire *well*.

BUSTING THE MYTH OF THE BUDGET

If you've ever sat down with the best intentions, fired up a budgeting app, and color-coded your monthly expenses down to the last latte, you probably felt a brief, delusional burst of control.

Then real life happened. Groceries went up. Again. The car needed tires. Again. Your kid's school sent home a flyer about a "mandatory" $300 field trip to a corn maze. And suddenly, your perfect budget was toast. You're not alone. In fact, very few people actually stick to a strict budget year in and year out. Why? Because human beings don't live in spreadsheets. They live in chaos, convenience, and Costco.

Numbers don't lie. A 2019 survey by the Certified Financial Planner Board of Standards (CFP Board), conducted with Heart+Mind Strategies, reveals that many Americans struggle with managing their household finances, regardless of income or assets.[6] Despite recognizing the benefits of budgeting, such as increased control, confidence, and security, many individuals find it challenging to implement and adhere to effective budgeting practices. Seventy-seven percent of respondents reported

---

[6] Certified Financial Planner Board of Standards, Inc. (CFP Board), "New Survey Shows Consumers, No Matter Their Income or Assets, Need Support with Spending, Household Budgeting," news release, January 24, 2019, accessed July 24, 2025, https://www.cfp.net/news/2019/01/new-survey-shows-consumers-no-matter-their-income-or-assets-need-support-with-spending-household-budgeting/

that it's easy to spend money. Sixty-four percent found it easy to overspend when using credit cards or mobile payments. Fifty-nine percent admitted they are not tracking their spending.

DO I NEED TO START INVESTING?

If you've ever seen a Reddit post titled something like *"YOLOed my student loans into Tesla calls—pray for me"*, you've already met the chaos that is WallStreetBets.

- ▶ It's the subreddit that launched a thousand headlines:
- ▶ A guy turned $50,000 into $48 million by betting on GameStop.
- ▶ Another put his life savings into AMC and filmed the rollercoaster in real-time.
- ▶ And let's not forget Dogecoin—literally a joke that minted millionaires.

This is the financial world's version of the Hunger Games, where FOMO (Fear of Missing Out) meets just enough luck to keep the rest of us irrationally hopeful. But it's the same thing as the person near you who just won the billion-dollar lottery. They were at the right place at the right time, and there is no lightning in a bottle that can guarantee the same results.

Here's the problem: these stories get clicks, not context. We never see the guy who bet his rent on crypto and lost it all. Or the folks who panic sold at the bottom, missed the rebound, and now spend their evenings Googling, *"Can you retire with regrets and $11,000 in an index fund?"* FOMO investing is seductive because it's fast, loud, and emotional. It makes you feel like if you're not doing something bold with your money, you're doing it wrong.

Real wealth doesn't come from viral moments. It comes from boring consistency. Nobody's posting TikToks about contributing to their Roth IRA for the fourteenth year in a row. But that's the person you actually want to be.

What's the point? You don't need to worry about investing nearly as much as you've been told. Yes, investing matters. Long-term growth matters. But obsessing over the rate of return, fees, and benchmarks while your financial life is on fire? That's like shopping for wallpaper while your kitchen is flooding.

The truth is, most people who fixate on investing don't even have the basics in place. And that's not a judgment, it's a pattern. We've seen people with $200,000 in their retirement accounts and $75,000 in credit card and car loan debt. Every month, they're earning seven percent in the market while paying twenty-one percent interest to Visa. That's not growth. That's financial cannibalism.

One of the most persistent myths in personal finance is that the rate of return is the holy grail of financial success. It's not. You don't need to beat the S&P 500. You don't need to chase a mythical ten percent average return. What you need is a plan. A target return that supports your actual life. If you're saving and investing fifteen to twenty percent of your income consistently, you don't need to swing for the fences. You can hit singles and still win the game.

Benchmark chasing is stressful, often misleading, and mostly irrelevant to your personal goals. A good financial plan doesn't rely on outperforming the market. It relies on outlasting your expenses.

IT'S TIME TO GET BETTER FINANCIAL ADVICE

Who do you get financial advice from?

When you were a child, your first financial decision probably dealt with a few dollar bills that you got under your pillow from the tooth fairy. You might have also gotten some advice from counselors, teachers, or your parents about paying for college. Your first boss might have encouraged you to start contributing to your 401(k). For most people, that's about it.

Where do you get financial advice from now?

Family, friends, coworkers. Or that one guy from your spin class who swears by crypto. You might even have a mentor who "retired early" and is now giving unsolicited money tips over brunch. And your friend who sold his IT business for $15 million is not in a position to give you any sort of advice. It's all well-meaning. It's also often *very* wrong. When you ask your cousin how he invests or your dad how he paid off the house early, you're getting secondhand advice based on someone else's situation, income, goals, and mistakes, not yours.

And the financial media? Not much better. Those pundits on TV yelling about index funds and gold bars? They're not trying to help you. They're selling ad space. They're entertainers, some with good hair, a few with fiduciary responsibility. So, who should you actually listen to? You probably need a solid financial planner to help you examine where you stand and where you want to go.

You wouldn't rewire your house based on a Reddit thread, and yet, that's how quite a few people approach their financial lives. They Google around, collect advice from friends and influencers, and hope the pieces magically fit together. The problem? Money isn't just about knowledge; it's about coordination. A real financial advisor doesn't just know how the parts work. They know how they work *together.*

Most people don't fail because they're lazy or reckless. They fail because they don't have a strategy. A financial planner helps you build one. They look at your whole picture: your income, debt, taxes, goals, risks, and stress levels, and design a plan that fits *your* life, not a generic blog post. The best planners don't sell you a product. They sell you confidence. And if you've ever lost sleep over money, you already know how valuable that is.

You can start with the basics. "Financial advisor" is a broad term. A financial planner, especially one with the CFP® (Certified Financial Planner™) designation, is someone who has been tested, vetted, and trained to help build actual financial plans. They shouldn't just try to sell you a list of products. They want to know what's going on with your spending habits, your goals, and your responsibilities so that they can help you make the most appropriate possible decision for you and your family.

Here's how to find someone who knows what they're doing and is the right fit for your life:

► **CREDENTIALS:** Look for a CFP® designation. That's not just alphabet soup. It means they've passed rigorous exams, and have real experience.

► **TRANSPARENCY:** They're willing to explain their fees, their process, and their own financial situation (yes, some even share their own plan, investments, and protection strategies).

> ► **PLAIN ENGLISH:** If you leave a meeting more confused than when you walked in, that's a red flag. A good planner can translate complex financial ideas into something that makes sense to you.

> ► **TRACK RECORD:** Use FINRA's BrokerCheck or the SEC's advisor search to look them up. You can see years of experience, disclosures, complaints, and any legal or financial red flags.

Here's what to watch out for so that you don't end up with bad advice.

> ► **LOTS OF JOB-HOPPING:** If an advisor has bounced between four or five firms in the last ten or fifteen years, ask why. It could be a sign they couldn't grow their business, or worse, that they were shown the door.

> ► **JUDGMENTS OR LIENS:** If someone is bad with their own money, it may not be best to let them near yours.

> ► **SALES OVER STRATEGY:** If all they talk about is products, like insurance, investments, or Roth conversions, but never ask about your goals, priorities, or current lifestyle, you're not getting a plan. You're getting a pitch.

Are you worried about your income and how a financial planner will look at your finances? Check the shame at the door. Most people don't show up feeling proud. They show up feeling embarrassed, behind, ashamed.

They walk in thinking:

"I should have started sooner."
"I make too much money to be this disorganized."
"I can't believe I maxed out a credit card just to go to my cousin's destination wedding."

You're not broken. You're just human. Money shame is everywhere. It's in the little voice that tells you you're not successful enough to need a financial plan. It's in the hesitation before opening your banking app. It's in the decision to put off meeting with someone because you think they'll judge you. But here's the truth: a good financial planner is not here to scold you; they're here to help you stop carrying all of this alone.

- ► You are not your credit score.

- ► You are not the student loans you took out when you were nineteen and just trying to make a decent life.

- ► You are not the bounced check, the budget that didn't work, or the 401(k) you forgot to roll over from that job you hated five years ago.

- ► You are a person who's trying. And that's all you need to start.

Financial shame keeps people stuck. It convinces them they must "fix everything" before they ask for help. But you don't go to a doctor only after you've healed yourself—and you don't need to get your finances "in order" before seeing a planner. In fact, the messier it is, the more valuable good guidance becomes. If you truly believe your finances are a mess, then you desperately need a planner with the necessary tools to get you back on track.

Another major blind spot? Thinking that financial planning is only for the wealthy. Here's an open secret. You don't need a million dollars to talk to a planner. You need a paycheck, a couple of goals, and the willingness to start. Unfortunately, many firms have positioned themselves as exclusive clubs. ("If you have over $500,000, give us a call!") That kind of gatekeeping keeps real people out of the planning process until it's too late. Good financial advice isn't about how much you have, it's about what you *do* with it.

So why should you spend money on a financial planner? Think of the people you love. Now think of the worst possible thing that could happen to those people. When someone is sick, or dying, or loses their job, will they be able to recover? Ask the average person if they have insurance, and they'll say yes. But dig a little deeper and you'll realize something critical: having something isn't the same as being covered. Most people assume their employer-provided benefits are enough. They're not. Employer coverage often has limits, loopholes, and expiration dates. It's a start, not a safety net.

Yes, you are *required* to insure your car and your house, but not your life or your income. Let that sink in. You can replace a vehicle. You can rebuild a home. But if something happens to *you*, the person generating the income, your family can't just "buy another one." Disability insurance, life insurance, and legal protections are foundational. Especially once you have kids, that's when financial planning becomes less about you—and more about who's depending on you.

CHAPTER 3

IN SEARCH OF A GOOD FILE CABINET

It happens more than you know. A new client walks in the door, wanting to get their finances in order. For the purposes of this book, we'll call this person "Dave."

Dave's a smart guy. Runs a small business, has two kids, a mortgage, and a Labrador that eats everything but kibble. Dave came to me to "get his financial house in order." I told him we'd start, as always, by gathering his documents, insurance policies, tax returns, and investment statements—the usual suspects.

"That should be easy," Dave said. "I'm pretty organized." Famous last words.

Two days later, I get an email: "Hey, I can't find my life insurance policy, but I know I have one. It's somewhere in my inbox or the bill cabinet, probably both. I'll find it this weekend."

One weekend turns into two. Then a month. Every call starts the same way: "Man, I've just been slammed. Work is crazy. The kids had soccer. We all came down with the swine flu. And my wife is dealing with so much right now."

At one point, he swears the document was in "a green folder in the kitchen drawer … or possibly in the garage." I picture his insurance policy huddled next to a box of mismatched Tupperware lids and the instruction manual for a 2009 vacuum cleaner. I'm certain he has it, because most people like Dave buy an insurance policy, but they almost never put it somewhere they can find it.

Finally, after weeks of hunting, Dave admits something important: "I'm not even sure I've *ever* seen the policy. I just remember someone selling it to me six years ago." So we end up calling insurance companies together to try to find a paper trail with Dave's name on it. Here's the thing: Dave is not unusual. Dave is *everywhere*. People *think* they're covered. They remember signing something. They assume that if something terrible happens, their family will be fine. But unless we have the actual policy, the details, the coverage amounts, and the beneficiaries, we're all just working off prayers and wishes.

Life is busy. But if your financial well-being depends on a single PDF buried under eight years of junk mail, it's time to hit pause and go digging. Nothing is more awkward than telling your spouse, "Good news! We're covered! Probably! I just can't prove it!" So do the future you a favor. Find the policy. Or call the company and get a new copy. Heck, let your financial planner help. But don't leave it in the Bill Cabinet of Doom, next to the expired coupons and old birthday cards. Your peace of mind deserves better than that.

Most people have a vague idea of their financial life. It can be difficult to keep track of everything—like pay stubs, junk drawers, what's left in the stored-mail box, emails, receipts, taxes, and investments. In your inbox is a retirement account you opened five years ago. Your insurance policies are buried in a PDF folder called "Taxes Maybe?" And when was the last time you read your pay stub? If that sounds like you, take a breath. You're not alone. But if you're serious about building a financial plan that works, step one is knowing where everything is.

A good financial advisor doesn't start with "Here's a product I think you should buy." They start with a full picture: What do you own? What do you owe? What insurance do you have? What benefits are hiding in your HR portal? Do you even know where your will is? Have you even made a will yet? If the person advising you *doesn't ask for your tax returns, insurance policies, pay stubs, investment statements, and legal documents,* then you don't have a financial planner. You have a salesperson who is interested in making money.

WHAT YOUR FINANCIAL PLANNER NEEDS FROM YOU

There is no world where you wave a wand and immediately get on top of your finances. No one can help you plan for your future if you don't know what's happening in your present. If your advisor isn't building your strategy around your actual financial documents, your real life, in real numbers, then they're making guesses. Those guesses are usually built to sell you something.

So here's where we start: gather your documents. All of them. The ones you forgot you had. The ones that are in a file folder in the closet. The ones from that job you left in 2016. If you want to get financially organized, this is the price of admission.

YOU NEED:

- ► At least two years of tax returns
- ► Your pay stubs
- ► All insurance policies (life, disability, home, auto, umbrella)
- ► Any benefits from work
- ► Investment account statements
- ► Wills, powers of attorney, and other legal documents
- ► Debt and loan statements
- ► Retirement account info (401(k)s, IRAs, etc.)

All this may sound too much, but it is the bare minimum required to see your whole financial picture clearly. If you don't know what you have, no one can help you protect, grow, or make it work harder for you. Many people will say they're "too busy" to do this. Sure, work, kids, errands, and life take time. But the real reason people avoid this step isn't time. It's usually one of two things: *shame* or *avoidance.*

They're embarrassed that they don't have it together. Or they're scared of what they'll see. But financial planning isn't about being perfect. It's about being honest. You don't have to have a pristine balance sheet. You just need to be willing to start. Once your financial life is organized, everything else becomes possible.

One of the first things I require from any client—and this is nonnegotiable—is that they fill out the first page of my intake questionnaire. It's straightforward: basic personal information, such as name, date of birth, address, Social Security number, and place of employment. From there, I ask them to gather every document on a detailed checklist—anything and everything they've got. That includes insurance policies, tax returns, pay stubs, investment account statements, employee benefits, and wills. If it touches their financial life, I want to see it.

If your current "financial planner" isn't asking for all of this, then you don't have a financial planner. You may have someone with a nice title and a polished pitch, but they're not building a plan—they're guessing. Suppose they're not examining your tax documents, reviewing your insurance coverage, understanding your benefits at work, or seeing your income and assets in detail. How could they possibly give you sound advice? They're flying blind.

What's worse, many of these so-called advisors are trained to ask just enough questions to figure out what you'll say yes to. They're framing their conversations in a way that leads you to tell them what to sell you. If you feel like you're being pitched a product in the first meeting or even the second, chances are, you are. That's not advice; that's sales.

Real financial planning takes time and information. It requires a complete picture of where you are, what you have, what you want, and what keeps you up at night. If someone starts suggesting solutions without knowing all that, they're not planning anything. They're just closing a deal. So, yes, you should have your documents, such as your last couple of years' tax returns, on hand, not just for your advisor, but for yourself. It's your life. You should know what's in it. You can't plan around a mess, but you *can* clean it up, and we will do that together.

HOW TO OVERCOME THE MENTAL BLOCK

It's easy to blame external forces for our financial stress: high taxes, rising interest rates, and inflation. And yes, those things matter. But much of our economic situation is shaped by our own behavior and the misinformation we've absorbed along the way.

Think about the typical financial advice most people follow. You get your first job, and what's the first thing you're told? *"Start contributing to your 401(k) immediately."* On the surface, that sounds responsible, but for many people, it's premature. The first two steps in any solid financial foundation aren't retirement contributions; they're *protection and liquidity.* Protecting yourself and your ability to earn an income, and building a saving account that you can actually access. These should be your top priority.

Instead, many people get stuck in a tug-of-war between two common maxims: "Max out your 401(k)!" and "Get out of debt!" And so they funnel every extra dollar into debt payments or retirement accounts, leaving nothing behind for themselves. What they don't realize is that they're sending all their cash flow out the door to banks, to credit cards, to investment firms, and leaving themselves with nothing to stand on when life inevitably throws a wrench into their plans.

Some things we know for sure: No one ever plans on getting sick. No one expects to get laid off, become disabled, or pass away prematurely. But these things happen. Your car might break down. Your roof might leak. And if you've built your financial life on the edge with no emergency savings and no protection in place, it only takes one stiff breeze to bring the whole thing crashing down.

Here's a little uncomfortable truth: most people spend more time planning their vacation than organizing their finances. Think about that. We'll dedicate hours to researching flights, arguing about rental cars, and browsing hotel reviews for a three-day getaway to Tuskaloosa. But ask someone to gather their insurance policies and last year's tax return? Suddenly, they've got a headache, three Zoom calls, and a deep, dark urge to take a nap before bed. Vacations are fun. Organizing your finances? Not so much.

There's also the shame factor. People say they're "too busy," but what they're really saying is:

- ► "I don't want to admit I have $5 in savings."
- ► "I know I don't have life insurance."
- ► "I've been meaning to set up a will, but I don't even know where to start."
- ► "I haven't contributed to my retirement account in years."
- ► "My passwords are a disaster, and I don't know where anything is."

If that's you, take a breath. You're human. Avoidance is normal. Shame is common. But neither of them will help you protect your future, put food on the table for your kids, or make sure your wife has an income in the event of your untimely demise.

The good news? It doesn't take much to turn things around. A normal person, yes, one just like you, can sit down for half an hour and make real progress. You don't need spreadsheets. You don't need a binder. You just need to find your stuff. Seriously. Half an hour. That's one episode of a Netflix show you won't even remember tomorrow. In that time, you could:

- ► Log in to your insurance provider's portal and download your policy.
- ► Pull your latest tax return from your inbox.
- ► Save a PDF of your most recent pay stub.
- ► Write down what accounts you know you have, even if you're not 100% sure what's in them.

If you think, "Well, I don't need to do that right now," ask yourself: If something happened to you tomorrow, would your loved ones know where to find any of it? Would your spouse know how to access your accounts? Would your kids have a way to get the money you thought you left behind for them? Would your family be grieving and financially stranded? You don't need to be perfect. You just need to be *prepared*. The only thing worse than financial stress while alive is leaving a financial mess behind when you're gone. So it's time to stop making excuses. You're not too busy. You're not too far gone. You don't need to be rich. You just need to start.

THE CHEATER'S GUIDE TO FINANCIAL ORGANIZATION

The dishes are done (or at least soaking), the kids are asleep (or pretending to be), and the house is finally quiet. This is your moment, the golden window between "parent mode" and "collapse on the couch mode." While it might not be your idea of a good time, this quiet half hour is one of the best opportunities you'll ever have to get financially organized.

Start small. Grab a notebook, your laptop, and maybe a glass of Pinot or Woodford on the rocks, whatever makes it feel less like work and more like reclaiming control. Your first job isn't to build a budget or determine your retirement timeline. *It's just to find your stuff.* Log in to your bank accounts, insurance portals, and retirement plans. Save PDFs or screenshots of what you can. Locate your last two years of tax returns. If it's all buried in your email, search for terms like "policy," "statement," or "1099." Don't worry about making sense of it all yet, just gather the puzzle pieces. If you have, or are thinking of, meeting with a planner, then they can help you make sense of it later.

Next, make a list. What accounts do you have? Where are your loans? Do you have life insurance through work, or did you mean to look into that three years ago? Write down everything you *know*, everything you *think* you have, and everything you've *completely forgotten about until just now*. This isn't about being perfect, it's about shining a flashlight into the corners of your financial life and seeing what's there. That alone will already put you ahead of most people.

Finally, take a breath. You don't have to organize your entire financial world in one night. But by taking that first step, by choosing to look, list, and gather, you've already started to move from reaction to intention. You're not just winging it anymore. You're building the foundation for a financial plan that fits your real life, not some spreadsheet fantasy. That means the next time a curveball hits (a broken water heater, a surprise medical bill, a school fundraiser with a $300 "suggested donation"), you won't feel like you're starting from scratch.

WHAT YOU SHOULDN'T ASK AN ADVISOR

A good financial advisor should be able to explain their philosophy clearly. No jargon. No cryptic charts. Just: "Here's how I think about money, and here's how I help people." You're on the right track if the explanation makes sense and it feels like a real conversation, not a sales pitch. But if someone's pushing products in the first meeting, rushing to "solve" your finances before they've even asked about your goals, that's not advice, it's a transaction.

Too many people also get stuck on the "how they get paid" question. Should you ask it? Sure. But don't lead with it like you're trying to catch a used car salesman in a lie. Most of the noise online about fee-only vs. commission-based vs. asset-under-management models is just … marketing. Every type of advisor needs to be paid somehow. The real question is: Do they put *your* needs first? Do they show you their process? Their own plan? Their actual thinking? If so, it matters less whether they're paid hourly or through fees, because the value isn't in the invoice. It's in the impact.

And if you're still skeptical, here's something to chew on: even the people who swear they can "do it themselves" usually end up paying *someone* eventually. DIY investors who pride themselves on using the lowest-cost funds at Vanguard often circle back a few years later, exhausted, confused, and ready to pay the one percent they tried so hard to avoid, just to make the stress stop. Managing finances can quickly become a second job, but one without a salary or a benefit attached. It's not failure. It's life. Financial planning is messy and nuanced, and sometimes you need a guide. Not to sell you something. But to walk with you through the process and help you see the whole picture.

You deserve a financial advisor who helps you *make sense* of your money, not just make moves with it.

WHAT NOT TO SAY AND WHY

▶ **"What's the hottest stock right now?"** This isn't Reddit or WallStreetBets. If you want gambling advice, go to Vegas. A good advisor builds a plan based on your goals, not headlines.

▶ **"Can you beat the market?"** Trying to "beat the market" is a losing game. What matters is whether your money is working toward your specific life goals, college, retirement, or travel, not whether it outpaced the S&P 500 last week.

▶ **"How much money do I need to start?"** You don't need to hit some magical threshold. You're ready if you're earning income and care about your financial future. Waiting until you "have enough" usually means you've waited too long.

▶ **"How do you get paid?" (Before you even know what they do)** It's not wrong to ask, but don't lead with this. Understand their process first. Without trust, how the planner gets paid won't matter anyway.

▶ **"Should I buy gold/crypto/dogecoin right now?"** If your financial plan depends on a trendy asset, you don't have a plan. You have hope, and maybe not even a prayer. Your advisor should help you build a sustainable, boring-on-purpose strategy.

► **"What's your rate of return?"** The planner is not an index fund. No advisor can promise performance; if they try, that's your sign to run.

► **"Can we skip the part about insurance?"** No, you cannot. If you care about your future and your family, protection isn't optional—it's foundational. If you're my client, it's mandatory.

► **"Can you just tell me what to invest in?"** Blind advice without context is dangerous. Without knowing your income, debts, goals, risk tolerance, and time horizon, it's not advice, it's malpractice.

► **"Do I really need all those documents?"** Yes. A real financial plan needs real data. If your advisor doesn't ask for your tax return, insurance policies, and paycheck stubs, *they're* doing it wrong.

► **"Can we meet once and call it a day?"** Financial planning isn't a onetime event—it's a lifelong process. If you're only in it for a quick fix, you're not looking for a planner. You're looking for a shortcut. And those rarely work.

CHAPTER 4

PROTECTING YOUR ASSETS

W hen you hear the phrase *"protect your assets,"* you probably immediately picture alarm systems, padlocked garages, car insurance, or maybe your annual checkup at the doctor's office. It makes sense because those are the kinds of protections we're taught to prioritize. But when it comes to your financial life, "asset protection" means something much more profound and far more essential.

But what if you don't own a million-dollar yacht or a condo in an up-and-coming neighborhood? Guess what? You don't have to be rich to have assets worth protecting. In fact, if you have a job, a family, a bank account, or a heartbeat, *you already do.* One of the most overlooked and most valuable assets any person has is their ability to earn an income. Your job, your skills, your experience, your education, and your professional certifications are all assets. They're what powers your financial engine and supports your family's future. You are their money machine.

Take a moment to think about this: if you earn $200,000 a year, that's two million dollars over the next decade, not including pay raises for inflation. A couple earning $300,000 combined and working steadily until age sixty-five could earn over $7 million in their working lifetimes. Most people never stop to consider their income potential as an asset, but if it were to suddenly disappear, due to illness, injury, or worse, the consequences would be immediate and life changing.

That's why the foundation of any sound financial plan starts with protecting the income stream. This means having adequate disability and life insurance, not just what your job throws in as a benefit. It means ensuring your assets are appropriately titled, sometimes through trusts, so they're shielded from lawsuits or probate nightmares. It means adding, when appropriate, an umbrella policy to help protect your home, savings, and investment from unexpected liability claims. It even means being thoughtful about where you keep your money, like 401(k)s and life insurance cash values, which often offer built-in legal protections depending on your state.

Protecting your assets isn't about hoarding wealth. It's about guarding the life you're building, piece by piece, paycheck by paycheck, so that one accident, lawsuit, or missed opportunity doesn't send it all crashing down. You've worked hard to get where you are. Now, you need to ensure that you don't lose everything.

WHY YOU NEED TO CONSIDER PAYING FOR PROTECTION

Paying for protection gets a bad rap, probably because most people picture Tony Soprano strolling into their office with a cigar and saying, *"Be a shame if something happened to that income of yours."* To be fair, in *The Sopranos*, "protection" usually meant giving up part of your paycheck so someone else didn't burn your place down.

But in the financial world, protection works a little differently. You do actually get something in return. Life insurance and disability coverage don't show up in a velour tracksuit and demand cash in a deli parking lot, scented with *gabagool*. They sit quietly in the background, waiting for the day when life takes a turn, and they could step in and help save your family from financial ruin. The mob may have offered "peace of mind" for a price, but your financial planner should offer it legally, ethically, and without a baseball bat. And honestly, isn't that the kind of muscle you want on your side?

So why do you want to pay more for something that may or may not happen later on? If you're feeling that way, you're not alone. Most people wonder the same thing until life throws them a curveball. Remember: we are all mortal, we are going to grow old, and at some point, we are all going to die. No amount of scientific progress guarantees that you will live forever in perfect health, despite the trials and tribulations of Brian Johnson on Netflix.

These facts make insurance seem like a seatbelt. You don't buckle up because you're *planning* on crashing, but you do it because you know accidents happen, and the risk of not being protected is too significant. The same logic applies to your income and your ability to work. For most people, your paycheck is your lifeline. It pays your mortgage, buys your groceries, fuels your retirement accounts, and takes care of your family. If that paycheck stops due to illness, injury, or something worse, what happens then?

Statistically, one in four working adults will experience a long-term disability during their career.[7] For many people, disability doesn't usually look like a catastrophic accident. It's not always crutches or wheelchairs. Most long-term disabilities are invisible, such as chronic illness, cancer, anxiety disorders, or neurological conditions. One of my clients, for example, can no longer work because looking at a screen triggers seizures. On the outside, they look perfectly fine. But their ability to secure an income is gone.

Employer-provided coverage is a start, but it's often not enough. Many people assume that just because they have *some* life or disability insurance through work, they're covered. But most of those policies are limited in scope and might only provide a fraction of what you'd need to maintain your lifestyle. And worse, they're tied to your employment. Lose your job, and you lose your coverage. Paying a small monthly premium now is about securing confidence. It's about working to ensure that, if something unexpected happens, you and your loved ones won't be scrambling to make ends meet. It's not just protection against disaster; it's a resilience plan. And that could be worth every penny.

---

[7]   Matt Messel, Tokunbo B. Oluwole, and David Rogofsky, "Public Knowledge About the Social Security Administration's Disability Programs: Findings from the Understanding America Study," *Social Security Bulletin* 82, no. 4 (2022): 1–33.

DOESN'T MY EMPLOYER HANDLE INSURANCE?

The average employed American generally gets insurance through their job. You get health insurance, life insurance, and in many cases, some sort of disability insurance. These offerings, should you choose to accept them, take a little out of your paycheck each month, and you probably never think about them once you've made your decision. This message will not self-destruct once you've read it, either. Guess what? It's still not enough in the event of an emergency. You don't install smoke detectors because you *plan* to have a fire. You don't wear a seatbelt because you *want* to crash. You do it because life is unpredictable, and when things go wrong, you don't want to be scrambling.

Employer-provided life insurance is a common benefit, but it often fails to offer comprehensive financial protection. Typically, these policies cover a flat amount or a multiple of your salary, which may not be sufficient for long-term needs such as mortgage payments, children's education, or daily living expenses. Moreover, such coverage is usually tied to your employment; leaving your job could mean losing this benefit.

Group life insurance provided through employers is generally low-cost because the coverage is basic and lacks customization. While it's a convenient benefit, these policies often don't offer valuable add-ons, known as riders, that can significantly improve your protection.

For example, many employer-sponsored plans exclude options like accelerated death benefits (which allow access to funds during a terminal illness), long-term care coverage, or the ability to convert a term policy into a permanent one. They also typically don't include protections like a waiver of premium if you become disabled or the ability to cover children under a separate term policy.

How much is a life worth? It's one of those questions that feels too big and too human to be answered with a spreadsheet. But back in 2001, a man named Kenneth Feinberg had to try. After the 9/11 attacks, the government put him in charge of the September 11th Victim Compensation Fund. His job? Decide how much money each grieving family should receive. There's a movie about it on Netflix called *Worth*. The movie is powerful, but it's also a reminder of something we rarely like to talk about: when tragedy strikes, there's always a dollar amount in the background. Not because people are greedy. Because money, whether we like it or not, is what pays the mortgage, the college tuition, and the medical bills. When a breadwinner dies unexpectedly, the ripple effects aren't just emotional. They're financial.

And that's why this story sticks with me. Feinberg had to create a formula, an actual equation, for how much someone's life was worth. He looked at age, income, dependents, future potential earnings … and he assigned each victim a number. But here's the uncomfortable truth: we all walk around with a number on our backs. We just don't like to think about it.

As a financial advisor, I'm not here to say what someone's life is worth emotionally or morally. That's not possible. But I do help people recognize their *economic* value, the income they generate for their families, the care they provide, the opportunities they make possible. If you're a parent with young kids, or someone who supports a partner or an aging parent, your ability to keep showing up and earning money might be the single most valuable thing in your household. And if that ability disappears because of an illness, injury, or something even worse, then what?

When I talk about human economic value, I'm not getting philosophical. I'm just talking about the value you bring to the table, plain and simple. It's the sum of your skills, your labor, your creativity, your knowledge, everything you do that contributes to the economy or the people around you. That could mean what you do for a living, how you generate income, or even how you innovate or solve problems in your community. It's not just about money in, money out. It's about what you create and the impact you have.

And here's the part that gets overlooked way too often: your value isn't just tied to a paycheck. Stay-at-home parents? Caregivers? Volunteers? They're all adding real, measurable value to the world, even if no one's cutting them a check for it. When we talk about building a financial plan, it must start with recognizing the unique value you bring and figuring out how to protect it, grow it, and utilize it to build the life you want.

But a group policy typically only pays out roughly one or two years' worth in salary, which probably wouldn't be enough for your family to stretch out.

Supplemental life insurance policies, which you can purchase independently, provide additional coverage to help bridge these gaps. These policies offer flexibility, allowing you to tailor coverage to your specific needs and circumstances. They also remain in effect regardless of your employment status, ensuring continuous protection for your beneficiaries.

During open enrollment periods, it's crucial to assess your life insurance needs comprehensively. Consider factors like your family's financial obligations, future expenses, and the adequacy of your current coverage. For many of us, it's tempting to brush it off: "I've got kids, bills, tuition, groceries ... now you want me to add *this*?"

But you have to remember that protection isn't about predicting the future. It's about preparing for the parts of it you *can't* predict. But even a modest amount of disability or life insurance you *own yourself* (not tied to your employer) gives you the power to say: *My family is going to be okay, even if something happens to me.* The question becomes, do you want them to be just okay, or would you rather rest comfortably knowing that they will be taken care of even if you're not there?

You chose to build a life, maybe with a spouse, kids, and a home. Choosing to protect that life isn't about fear. It's about love, responsibility, and being the kind of person your family can count on, no matter what.

But insurance isn't something you can just put off until later. Getting life insurance and disability insurance becomes more difficult and expensive the older you get, and even harder if you have health issues or risky habits like DUIs or smoking, or Zyns, or any kind of tobacco habit. Unlike buying stocks, which you can do from jail, life insurance requires you to be insurable. That means qualifying based on age, health, and lifestyle. The younger and healthier you are when you apply, the better your chances of getting a solid policy at an affordable premium. That's why financial professionals recommend locking in coverage as early as possible. You can't predict what health issues or life changes might come up over the next thirty years, and you can't buy insurance after you already need it. Once the moment is gone, it's gone for good.

In my two decades of experience, no beneficiary has ever complained that the life insurance payout was too generous. In fact, due to inflation, many find it *still* isn't enough.

HOW CAN I PROTECT MY ASSETS?

True asset protection is more strategic and nuanced than just physical security. You need to fully understand what you own, what it's worth, and how vulnerable it might be. Income is one of the most overlooked assets, yet it's often the most valuable.

Beyond income, your assets may include savings accounts, investment portfolios, your home, and even intellectual property or side businesses. Many of these are exposed to risks you might not expect, including lawsuits, divorces, medical issues, or even cases of online slander. Something as fundamental as having the wrong auto or home insurance policy, or skipping an umbrella policy, can lead to devastating financial exposure. Yet, nine out of ten people skip that coverage. Worse still, many entrepreneurs and side hustlers enter new ventures without the proper legal structure or liability coverage, thereby putting their assets, such as their home or savings, directly at risk.

There are several ways to help build a financial "fortress" around what you own. Asset protection trusts are a great option in certain states. They move your money out of your name and into a trust that a third party controls. It may sound complex, but it's a powerful tool for protecting money from lawsuits or creditors. Business owners might consider borrowing against receivables or stripping out equity from valuable properties and placing that money into protected assets like annuities (depending on your state laws). Don't overlook the old-school methods: maximize your retirement account contributions, keep business and personal assets separate, and get an umbrella insurance policy. That last one can save you significant time if someone slips on your icy driveway and sues.

A strategic plan includes much more than just having insurance. It involves the correct titling of accounts, utilizing trusts to protect inheritances from lawsuits or divorces, updating wills and powers of attorney, and ensuring beneficiary designations match your estate plans. All of this may sound like work, and it is. However, not doing it leaves your financial future and the future of those you provide for at the mercy of chance.

Can you risk waiting until you're ready to do it? Well, not really. As one advisor put it, if you were going to do it on your own, it'd already be done. That's why working with a financial planner who advocates for comprehensive asset protection, before life's unexpected events occur, is so crucial. Because once a lawsuit is filed, or a health issue arises, or a relationship ends, it's too late to go back and put up the safety net. Strategy is everything.

CALM YOUR ANXIETY WITH THESE SEVEN QUESTIONS

Asset protection isn't just about locking things away. It involves being proactive, smart, and strategic. When you're working with a financial advisor, here are some key questions to ask to make sure your financial life is shielded from life's "what-ifs."

1. **What are my most valuable assets, and which ones are most at risk?** Your advisor should help you identify more than just your house or bank accounts. Think income, retirement accounts, business interests, and even your ability to earn a living. Ask which ones could be vulnerable in a lawsuit, divorce, or emergency, and how to protect them.

2. **Do I have enough insurance, and is it the appropriate kind?** Basic employer coverage is often not enough. Ask about life insurance, disability insurance, umbrella policies, and long-term care options. Make sure you understand the limits, exclusions, and whether your policies will follow you if you change jobs.

3. **Should I consider a trust or different account titling?** Ask whether a revocable or irrevocable trust might make sense for your situation. Proper titling of bank accounts, property, and investments can help shield your assets from probate, creditors, and messy legal disputes later.

4. **Are my retirement accounts and investments protected from lawsuits or bankruptcy?** Not all accounts are created equal. Some retirement plans (like employer-sponsored 401(k)s) offer more protection than individual IRAs. Ask which accounts have the most legal safeguards, and how much you should be contributing to those.

5. **What are the risks I haven't thought of?** A good advisor should bring up the "what ifs" you're not even considering: side business liability, car accidents, online slander, divorce, or illness. Ask them to stress test your plan and look for gaps.

6. **What does my estate plan say, and is it aligned with my financial plan?** Your will, powers of attorney, and healthcare directives should be aligned with your asset protection strategy. Ask your advisor to review them and coordinate with your attorney, so everything works together.

7. **How often should we review my protection strategy?** Life changes. Jobs change. Families grow. Ask your advisor how often you should revisit your protection strategy and what life events should trigger a review. It doesn't have to be every day, but it should be more than once a decade.

TWO ORANGES PLUS TEN YEARS EQUALS ONE BIG STAIN

If I put two oranges on a coffee table and leave them there, even in a plastic container that is supposed to protect them from the elements, it won't matter in ten years. If you put any fruit or vegetable in a safe for ten years, you will end up with a stain, not the fruit.

What does this have to do with the price of eggs? You can't stop inflation. It's a constant force in the economy, like gravity, always pulling at the value of your money, year after year. Prices go up, purchasing power goes down. So the goal isn't to *block* inflation. The goal is to take reasonable measures to keep an asset in its best shape, but when it's time to move on, it's time to move on.

That means your strategy has to go beyond simply saving. Stashing cash under the mattress or even just keeping it in a regular bank account is a guaranteed way to let inflation quietly eat away at your wealth. Over time, the money you worked so hard to save won't stretch nearly as far. What costs $100 today might cost $120 in just a few years.

The antidote? Smart investing. When you put your money to work in assets that have historically outpaced inflation, such as stocks, real estate, or even certain types of bonds, you give yourself a fighting chance. You're not just saving; you're growing. And that growth is what helps you maintain (or even increase) your financial power over time. In that sense, investing is a form of asset protection—because it protects what your money can *do* for you, not just the money itself.

So yes, you can't lock inflation out of the room, but you can outrun it with the right plan. And that plan should begin as soon as you start thinking seriously about your financial future. One of the most effective ways to beat inflation is by investing in the stock market. Over time, stocks have historically returned 7–10% annually, which far outpaces the average inflation rate of 2–3%.

Tangible assets like real estate and commodities (such as gold) also tend to rise in value during inflationary periods, making them another solid option. At the same time, don't overlook the impact of paying off high interest debt; eliminating a credit card with a 15% interest rate is essentially like earning a 15% return, risk-free. Increasing your income through continuing education or acquiring in-demand skills can also help you outpace inflation on the earning side.

Asset protection isn't just for the ultra-wealthy or people with seven-figure portfolios. It's for anyone who has something to lose. One of the most practical steps you can take, outside your 401(k) at work, is to get your accounts titled properly and to set up your basic legal documents. A will. A power of attorney. A healthcare directive. Maybe a trust. And yes, I know it's easy to say, "We'll get around to that later," but honestly? You won't. No one ever *wants* to do this stuff. You're not going to wake up one Saturday and feel excited about filling out beneficiary forms and digging up last year's tax return. But this is exactly why working with a real financial planner matters: someone who will not only remind you to do it, but walk you through the process and connect you with attorneys and professionals who can make it happen.

Now, if you're the kind of person who's been procrastinating on these steps, I get it. Life happens. But while you wait, you're getting older. Maybe less healthy. No one plans to get sick, lose a job, or pass away early. But every week, I meet people who assumed they had more time, and now they're scrambling. You don't want to be in that position.

When it comes to trusts, let's demystify the basics. A *revocable trust* keeps your assets in your estate and gives you control, but offers limited protection. An *irrevocable trust*, on the other hand, moves those assets out of your estate entirely. You can't be the trustee, and it's not "your" money anymore, but it *is* protected from lawsuits, divorce, long-term care costs, and creditors. A lot of my wealthier clients use irrevocable trusts to quietly set up inheritances that are protected for their kids, without the awkwardness of prenups. It's smart planning. Quiet planning. And it's available to more people than you'd think.

Don't overlook the titling of your accounts, either. How something is titled—whether it's in your name, jointly with a spouse, or in a trust—has real legal consequences. And those rules change by state. Joint tenancy might protect you better in one state, while a trust could be smarter in another. This is why working with someone who actually *knows your state's laws* and *asks for your documents* is critical.

Review the answers to the seven questions above, and if you answered "no" to any of the questions, then you don't have a plan. You have a patchwork. And patchworks don't hold up in a storm.

CHAPTER 5

A TALE OF DEBT, MINIMUM PAYMENTS, AND MAXIMUM REGRET

I t's a normal day for Josh, our typical working dad. He leaves his wife early at 6:00 a.m. and drives to work in a car that could use an upgrade, but works well enough for now. All he makes goes to rent, bills, and student loans from the past. His wife wakes up a little later to take their three-year-old to daycare and then heads to work herself. Her income goes to her student loans, maintaining their older SUV, and paying for daycare.

Josh comes home from work to find his wife and child waiting for him. "Guess what, honey?" his wife announces. "We're pregnant again!"

While Josh can't help but be happy about the new addition to the family, he isn't sure that he's going to be able to afford a new car to carry the family around, a new home with another bedroom for the second child, and *another* childcare bill.

Furthermore, his wife is going to be out of work for a little bit while she carries the baby and cares for it after birth.

A few weeks later, Josh discovers a flat tire on that car. He has to take out a payday loan online to cover the cost of a new tire, which puts him in even more debt. In desperation, Josh now has to prioritize the higher-interest debt over the student loans, obtain a forbearance on the student loans, and ends up adding more interest to what he owed.

How could Josh have attacked this situation differently? Real financial progress doesn't come from extremes. It comes from balance. A good financial advisor can help you find innovative ways to reduce or eliminate debt *while* growing your assets. Because if your whole plan is to pay everything off first and *then* start investing "someday," that's not a plan, it's wishful thinking. You can't build wealth on wishes and good vibes alone.

Student debt is a common phenomenon, especially for those who wish to have better-paying jobs. Credit card debt and payday loan debt are a close second, with higher interest rates and predatory approaches.

WHY YOU NEED TO STOP WATCHING FINANCE TALK SHOWS

Most people do not major in finance or have the experience to be their own financial advisors. So, where do most people go? Chances are you connect with a newsletter, a video channel, or a cable news network and hope you'll get good advice there. You can feel comforted or inspired by TV-ready soundbites: *"Pay off all your debt!"* or *"Never use a credit card!"* But there's a big difference between what works for television ratings and what works for your personal financial life.

Many of these so-called experts no longer hold professional licenses. Why? Because issuing blanket financial advice to millions of people opens the door to massive liability. That's why, if you watch their shows all the way through or skim the fine print on their books and courses, you'll often see disclaimers that their advice is for "entertainment purposes only." In reality, they're not offering personalized planning. They're selling programs, promoting books, and generating ad revenue.

There's nothing wrong with inspiration. But don't confuse one-size-fits-all advice with actual financial planning. Your situation, your debts, your income, your goals, and your family are unique. The smartest financial moves often involve nuance, trade-offs, and strategy, rather than absolutes. So, listen if you want, but don't treat finance celebrities as your advisor. They don't know your life. A real financial professional does.

THE TRUTH ABOUT PAYING OFF DEBT

We've all heard it somewhere, especially from well-meaning family, friends, and internet gurus, that you have to pay off all your debt before doing anything else. It sounds responsible. It sounds logical. But in the real world? It often just doesn't hold up.

Chances are you've already experienced this problem. The moment you think you're finally close to wiping out your debt, *life happens*. The roof starts leaking. The car breaks down. A kid gets a terrible injury or illness. Daycare bills kick in. That clean slate you were working toward suddenly disappears under a pile of new, necessary expenses. So if your entire financial plan depends on reaching zero debt before saving or investing, you're building on quicksand.

That's why a better approach is one that's *coordinated*, not reactive. For many people, especially those with limited cash in the bank, it can make more sense to pay just the minimums on debt while focusing on building an emergency fund. Then, once or twice a year, make lump sum payments toward your balances. This way, you're building financial stability *and* attacking debt in an innovative, structured way, without leaving yourself exposed to the next unexpected expense.

And about that advice to pay off your mortgage as fast as possible? Ask yourself where it came from. Chances are it wasn't from a credentialed financial advisor; it was from Uncle Joe, your coworker's cousin, or a TikTok video creator who was paid to recommend a product. While some of that advice has merit, it's not one-size-fits-all. Strategy beats speed when it comes to debt, and a good financial planner can help you find the right balance.

Isn't paying off your mortgage early a good idea? No, it's not, for many reasons. When people talk about paying off their mortgage as fast as possible, they're often relying on advice handed down from parents or grandparents. But here's the thing: mortgages in the 1960s, '70s, and '80s were *very* different from what we have today.

30 YEAR FIXED MORTGAGE RATE (1971-2026)

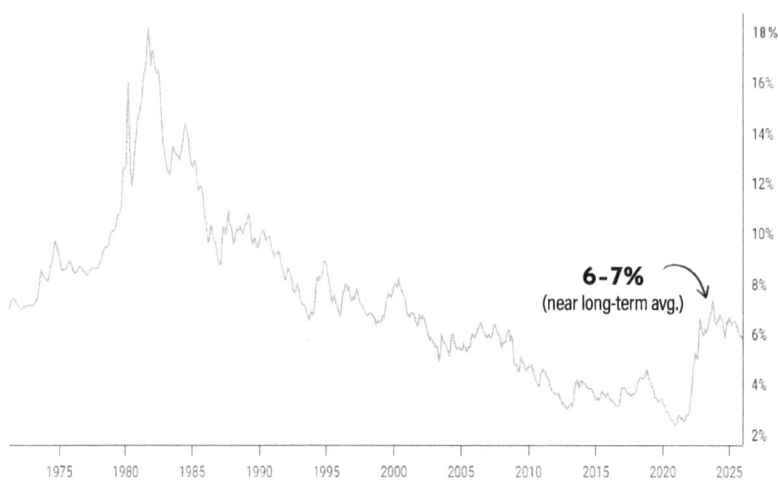

SOURCE: Adapted from Macrotrends, "30 Year Fixed Mortgage Rate (1971–2026)," accessed January 26, 2026.

Back then, interest rates could range from 14–20%. In that environment, aggressively paying down your mortgage made financial sense because you were burning cash on interest. But today? A mortgage rate of 6–7% might feel high compared to the historically low rates of the last decade, but it's right around the historical average. If your current rate is in that range, it might be wiser to simply make your regular payments and use your extra cash to invest, save, or build an emergency fund. Yes, depending on your tax situation, some people can still deduct a portion of their mortgage interest, which can offset some of the cost. The key? There's no one-size-fits-all answer. Blanket advice doesn't help much if it's based on someone else's financial reality from forty years ago.

The real reason many people feel like they can't afford to buy a home today often isn't the interest rate. It's the down payment. If you haven't spent the past several years saving diligently, or if you stretched for a house outside your actual affordability range, it's going to catch up with you. Too many people fall into the trap of thinking they "deserve" the dream home, the new car, the upgraded lifestyle as soon as they land a high paying job. But what you really deserve is the financial security your income can create, *if you manage it well.* Buying more house than you can maintain, skipping the emergency fund, or piling on luxury expenses can leave you worse off than when you were a broke student. That's not progress, that's a trap.

ARE YOU GOOD DEBT OR BAD DEBT?

People love to draw hard lines between "good" and "bad" debt, and while there's truth in those labels, it's not always black and white. Generally speaking, high interest consumer debt, such as credit cards, is considered bad debt. It costs more than it helps. But some debt, like a fixed rate mortgage, student loans, a security-backed line of credit, or business loans, can be strategic tools for growth.

A mortgage, for instance, can allow you to build equity while keeping your housing costs relatively stable. Mortgages can be used to get a deduction on your taxes. Even student debt, if used wisely, is an investment in your earning potential. The key is structure. You have to know what you're signing up for and ensure it aligns with your financial goals.

If you pay off your mortgage too early, and the roof leaks or you need to replace the entire basement floor, you can't just pull the bricks out of your home to pay the bills. There are new ordeals that come into play when you kiss your mortgage goodbye.

But what if you signed up for a super-predatory student loan when you were a teenager? Don't you have to pay off that bad debt immediately, so that you can survive? Even bad debt can be managed smartly. You don't always have to follow the all-or-nothing approach popularized by media personalities. Sometimes, refinancing or restructuring your loans can create breathing room in your budget and make debt more manageable.

A good financial advisor will help you explore your options before you panic. Remember, personal finance is personal. What works for someone else might not work for you. Blanket advice may sound motivating, but a proper strategy takes nuance.

STAY OUT OF DEBT BY PREPARING FOR THE WORST

One of the most common missteps in personal finance is putting all your money into accounts that are inaccessible, such as retirement plans, long-term investments, or locked up savings, without having anything left for everyday life. That might sound responsible on paper, but in the real world, it's a recipe for debt. When the car breaks down, the roof leaks, or tuition bills show up, you're left turning to credit cards, home equity lines, or student loans, not because you mismanaged, but because you weren't liquid.

Financial stress usually starts early when you're juggling part-time jobs, classes, and budgeting without a safety net. For many people, that stress never fully goes away. So, managing debt isn't just a mathematical problem; it's also a mental health and self-care issue.

If you have a family, dependents, or even just a spouse, there's another perspective on paying off debt. It might feel virtuous to throw every spare dollar at your debt. But when you have people depending on you, that approach can quickly turn from responsible to reckless. Life doesn't pause because you're trying to be debt free. If your child breaks a leg and needs medical care, if your elderly parent has a sudden health emergency, or if the family car dies on the way to school drop-off, none of those situations can be fixed with a paid-off credit card. What they require is liquid, accessible, ready to use money.

Once you use your capital to pay off a loan, that money is gone. You can't get it back without applying for more credit, and that may come at a worse interest rate, or not at all if your circumstances change.

Financial security means more than zeroing out balances; it means being prepared for the unexpected. When you've got a spouse, kids, or aging parents counting on you, having an emergency fund is not a luxury—it's a responsibility. In many cases, keeping cash on hand is worth more than having a debt free record, because it lets you respond, adapt, and stay afloat when life happens.

WHEN IT MAKES SENSE TO GO INTO DEBT

The world runs on credit and interest, so as you're aware, you cannot live without having some kind of credit score. Taking out a few small credit cards makes sense as long as you can pay back what is owed over time without causing your family or life to suffer. Taking out a student loan to gain more knowledge in your chosen field will inevitably lead to a higher salary and more job security. That kind of debt is necessary to continue to thrive, and therefore, it is worth it.

Similarly, borrowing to start or expand a well planned business can open the door to higher income and long-term financial stability. These types of debt are about leveraging money today to create opportunities tomorrow.

Let's talk about Securities-Backed Lines of Credit, or SBLOCs. The basic pitch sounds great: instead of selling your investments when you need cash, you just borrow against them. Keep your portfolio intact, tap into some liquidity, and move on with your life. Sounds smart, right? Well, here's the deal. SBLOCs can be useful tools *in the right situation*, but they're also loaded with risks that most people don't fully understand. These things are marketed hard by brokerage firms because they make money on the interest you're paying. So the advice isn't always coming from a place of objectivity.

Here's how it works. You use the stocks, bonds, or mutual funds in your investment account as collateral to open a line of credit. It's kind of like a home equity line, but instead of your house, you're putting your investments on the line. You make interest-only payments every month, and you can borrow, repay, and borrow again, like a revolving credit line.

But there's a catch. If the market takes a dip and the value of your portfolio drops, your lender can hit you with a maintenance call, or a demand to either put more money in or pay back part of the loan *fast*, usually within a couple of days. If you don't? They can start liquidating your investments to cover the difference. That's right: *they* sell *your* securities, possibly at a loss, and you don't get a say about when or how.

And remember, these are non-purpose loans, which means you can't use the funds to buy more investments. You can use it for pretty much anything else: buying a house, funding a business, paying tuition—but not to trade stocks.

In terms of credit limits, you can typically borrow anywhere from fifty percent to ninety-five percent of your account value, depending on what kinds of assets you hold. But lenders usually want to see a portfolio worth at least $100,000 before they'll even talk to you. They may not run a credit check because they're just looking at your investments, but don't confuse that with low risk.

And yes, interest rates on these loans can be lower than personal loans or credit cards, especially if rates are relatively tame. But that interest is calculated daily and can fluctuate with market rates (like the SOFR "Security Overnight Financing Rate" or the prime rate), which means your cost of borrowing can change month to month. You might get an option for a fixed rate, but not always.

Bottom line? If you've got a large, diversified, and relatively stable portfolio and a short-term cash need, and you fully understand the risks, an SBLOC *might* make sense. But if you're using it to fund your lifestyle or a side hustle, or you're stretching just to qualify, then it's probably a bad idea. Because when the market turns (and it always does), these loans can unravel fast.

Debt also makes sense when it's used to acquire appreciating assets. Taking out a mortgage to buy a home, for instance, allows you to build equity over time while providing a place to live. The same applies to investment properties that can generate steady rental income—if managed wisely, this kind of borrowing can create wealth rather than erode it. Even credit cards, often seen as risky, can help you build a solid credit history when used responsibly and paid off on time.

There are also times when going into debt is simply the most practical option. Financing a reliable vehicle so you can get to work or covering unexpected medical bills are examples where debt might be necessary to maintain your quality of life. In these situations, preserving liquidity is key. Instead of using all your available cash to pay off debt aggressively, keeping a financial cushion ensures you can handle emergencies without falling further into debt. The key is having a plan: debt should support your financial goals, not derail them.

What isn't worth it is "keeping up with the Joneses." No one deserves to have new cars each year or designer clothes just because they feel behind. Taking on debt to maintain a lifestyle you can't afford is a trap, and it's one that's easy to fall into when you're comparing your life to others, especially on social media. Yes, we know: your neighbors, friends, coworkers, and characters on Netflix that are supposed to be representative of you have it, so why can't you? If the purchase doesn't contribute to your long-term stability, earning potential, or well-being, then it's probably not worth going into debt for. You'll only spend months stressing over paying that debt back.

HUSTLING EVERY DAY– RIGHT INTO THE GRAVE

You've probably seen it online or on television. People keep looking for ways to make extra cash on the side so that they can pay off their debt. But here's the problem: you're only making the situation worse if you have a main job plus however many side hustles you decide to take on. Doubling down on a job with better pay and long-term growth potential is often more sustainable and more effective than trying to work seventy-hour weeks between multiple gigs.

Side hustles come with hidden costs. Sure, they may bring in a little extra money, but they also eat up your time, energy, and mental bandwidth. That's time you could be spending with family or resting, both of which are essential for your long-term health.

And burnout? It's real, and it's expensive. Whether you're a gig worker or a young professional moonlighting after hours, the stress of overworking often leads to physical health issues, relationship strain, and ultimately, more financial problems. The smarter path is to build a career that sustains you, not one that forces you to keep borrowing time from your life to pay off your debt.

A side hustle might seem like a quick fix when you're drowning in debt, but it can quietly sabotage the very thing that's going to help you build lasting wealth: your career. Your primary job is usually where you'll have the most significant potential for raises, promotions, benefits, and long-term stability. But when your energy is drained from working late nights or weekends on a side hustle, your performance at your primary job can suffer. You're not as sharp in meetings. You don't have the bandwidth to take on new projects. You miss chances to stand out and move up. If you're in healthcare, working *locum tenens* can really take a toll on your ability to make crucial decisions. You open yourself up to more risks, and those risks can be *expensive.*

That's the hidden cost of hustling on the side: it can stall or even damage your long-term earning power. Most people don't build real wealth from Uber shifts or Etsy shops. They do it through focused effort, advancement, and strategic growth in their careers. If you burn yourself out chasing pennies outside your 9-to-5, you might miss the chance to earn real dollars where it counts most. Protect your time, guard your energy, and invest in the thing that will pay you back the most over time: your profession.

FOOD FOR THOUGHT

If you spend any time scrolling TikTok, LinkedIn, or whatever we're calling Twitter now, you'll run into these rants about Social Security. They usually go something like, "I paid X amount into Social Security, and the government's only going to give me Y back in retirement? If I had just invested that money myself, I'd be a millionaire by now. It's theft!" But here's what people don't realize: half of the money that went into Social Security *wasn't yours to begin with.* It came from your employer. That's right: only half of those payroll taxes came out of your paycheck. The other half came out of your employer's pocket. So no, it's not just "your" money.

And honestly, if we're talking about fairness, maybe we should be thanking employers for making those contributions at all. Sure, they're required to by law, but it's still money going into a system that's meant to support you later in life. The idea that you could have invested all of it on your own and turned it into some massive pile of cash sounds great in theory, but let's not forget: there's no guarantee on investment returns. None. That hypothetical nine percent return? It's just that: hypothetical.

It's the same thing we see with health insurance. Many people are unaware that their employer often covers half, or sometimes even more, of those premiums. Just because you're not seeing that money directly doesn't mean it's not benefiting you. Social Security works the same way. It's a shared system. And while it's far from perfect, pretending it's all your personal investment fund just isn't the reality.

CHAPTER 6

YOUR PLAN SOUNDS GREAT-BUT WILL IT WORK?

"**L**ook," Dan says, sipping his $7 nitro cold brew with the confidence of a man who's read *The Millionaire Next Door* twice. "I've got a Roth IRA, a 401(k) with a match, and I only carry one credit card with travel points. I'm basically a financial ninja." Dan's coworkers hear this song and dance almost every business day, somewhere between 9:00 a.m. and 5:00 p.m. It's a pity that bragging to your coworkers doesn't count as reprehensible behavior in the workplace.

To anyone who listens to Dan, it might be easy to believe that he has everything covered. He'll be able to retire, he'll be able to make the most out of his income, and he'll be able to cover all his expenses, right?

Then Dan checks his bank account and realizes he has $238.74 until payday, three subscriptions he forgot to cancel, and an emergency fund that could maybe cover the cost of a single tire … but not the car attached to it. Dan is all of us. He has access to the best information available from a Google search or an inspirational, AI-generated financial pep talk. However, he still isn't quite able to put everything into practice. What can Dan do differently to make better sense of his financial situation?

It's one thing to memorize every pithy piece of financial wisdom. "Pay yourself first!" "Live below your means!" "The stock market always goes up in the long run!" But it is quite another to weave those rules into a life that's, well, messy. Because life isn't a checklist—it's daycare bills, broken appliances, unexpected vet visits, and moments of stress shopping on Amazon that no budget app could predict.

If you're playing on a baseball team, stepping up to the batter's box might seem very simple. You just have to hit the ball out of the park, right? But every single pitch thrown is going to be different. You can't just swing in the same textbook style every time and expect to connect with the ball. And even if the pitcher doesn't throw the ball correctly, the umpire might still argue that it's in the strike zone. It all depends on the circumstances.

Dan, bless him, isn't dumb or unaware. He's just stuck in the space between *knowing* and *doing*. He's the kind of guy who sets up automatic transfers into his Roth IRA, but then forgets to budget for groceries and ends up Venmo-requesting his co-workers for lunch money. He's got the right ideas—save, invest, budget—but hasn't quite translated them into a system that works *with* his life, not *against* it.

Unless you have a degree in advanced finance, you are probably dealing with the same issue. You can scroll through TikTok and hear five different gurus give five conflicting opinions about what to do with your next $500. One says pay down debt, one says buy Bitcoin, one says start a vending machine business. Meanwhile, Dan's still trying to remember the password to his budgeting app, for which he pays $8.00 a month and almost never uses. (Maybe it's time to dump that app, Dan.)

The problem isn't education. It's integration. Until your financial plan fits the rhythm of your actual life, it's just noise. What Dan needs isn't another finance book. He needs a framework that leaves room for late-night Uber Eats, medical co-pays, and a boss who hasn't given him a raise since 2019. He needs balance, not just ambition. He needs a system that lets him *live* while still making progress, because the perfect plan you can't follow is worse than the imperfect one you can.

FIND YOUR PATH WITH A FINANCIAL ADVISOR

Everyone knows the theory behind good financial habits: budget your spending, eliminate unnecessary debt, save consistently, and invest wisely. However, much like Dan, life tends to happen outside of spreadsheets and budgets. If Dan had walked into my office and told me he was actually ready to put his money to work, then we might have had a deeper conversation.

One of the first things I do when working with a new client is dig into their actual cash flow. I review their debt structure, their tax returns, their recurring expenses, and everything else that's pulling money out of their account each month. Often, I can find cash flow that they didn't even realize they had.

Why? Because it has been quietly accruing interest payments, or fees, for financial institutions that were more than happy to collect them.

Once we recover that lost cash flow, I won't let it fall back into the same old traps. I set up an automated savings plan, but not in a regular checking or savings account, where it's easy to just move money around at will. Rather, we funnel those dollars into an account that I can monitor alongside them. It adds just enough accountability that people stop and think before making impulse purchases.

It's a little like having someone peeking over your shoulder when you're about to click "add to cart." In a way, this method helps to stop you before you make those massive purchases that might not age well later on. You won't be cash poor with an expensive car you can't afford to maintain. You also won't need those credit cards to serve as an emergency fund because you'll have an actual emergency fund to lean on.

From there, we slowly turn up the dial. As debts get paid off or salaries increase, we boost that automated savings percentage bit by bit, until we're hitting that magic number: 20% of gross income saved. It's not a sprint, and it doesn't happen overnight. But it's systematic and sustainable. That's what putting theory into practice looks like: thoughtful, adaptive, and grounded in your actual life, not in financial fantasyland.

Sometimes I meet with people who *technically* have all the pieces in place: they've got an advisor, they're maxing out their 401(k), they're putting money into a brokerage account, like Vanguard, Robinhood, Charles Schwab, you name it. They've built up a nice little nest egg. However, upon closer examination, I see that they're also juggling multiple car payments, credit card balances, and lingering student loans that are draining their monthly cash flow, with little to no protection in place. That's when I suggest something most people don't expect: sell off some of that investment portfolio, eliminate those debts, and then redirect the freed up cash flow *back into* investing. It's not a step backward, it's a more innovative way forward.

Say you've got a $1,000/month car payment and still owe $20,000 on the loan. If you can pay that off with your brokerage account, you instantly recover $12,000 a year in cash flow. Compare that to the $20k you might have invested at Schwab.

Suddenly, you're "investing" in your monthly freedom, and it's a better return than the market. That $1,000/month now gets automated into your investment account, and because it's no longer going out the door in debt payments, it builds momentum quickly. This is what I mean by cash flow optimization. It's not just about what you earn, but what you keep and *reuse intentionally.*

Now, let's talk about impulse spending and what I like to call the "life keeps happening" excuse. Emergencies aren't a personal curse. They happen to *everyone.* So when people tell me, "This always happens to me," I offer a little tough love: "No, this happens to *all of us.* But some choose to fix it." That's why I keep savings in an account that *isn't* with their local bank. Psychologically, it makes a difference when someone knows I can see what's going on. It creates real accountability. We aim to automate savings at 20% of gross income and let the rest flow back into life. If you make $100,000 a year, that's $20,000 saved, and you still get to spend $80,000. You're telling me you can't live on $6,666 a month?

If that's difficult, then yes, it might be time to consider selling the car. Buy used instead of new. Move to a more affordable residence. These aren't punishments; they're survival strategies, and eventually you would have had to resort to these actions anyway, especially if you're already living outside of your means.

Budgeting doesn't work for most people. It's too strict or too soft, and both lead to failure. What does work is flipping the logic: save first (automatically), then spend what's left. And no, you don't need to constantly change your plan unless you've had a significant life shift. Your financial plan should have a solid foundation: protect what you have, save 20%, and enjoy the other 80%. It's not glamorous, but it works.

GIVE YOUR PLAN SOME TIME TO WORK BEFORE CHANGING IT

One of the most damaging habits I observe, fueled by media hype and some popular celebrity advisors, is the tendency to constantly tweak, tinker, and "optimize" one's financial plan. You've probably heard it before: "Review your finances regularly," "Adjust your strategy," "Be flexible!" That advice sounds responsible, even proactive. However, it often leads to chaos. Constantly shifting directions in your financial plan is not only unnecessary, it can be outright destructive.

Let's break this down. A real financial plan accounts for your short-term, mid-term, and long-term goals. Once those goals are mapped out, you're saving appropriately, and your risk protections are in place, any change you make from there should be *meaningful*. Not emotional. Not based on some new TikTok guru or cable finance personality. If you're constantly jumping at every market dip or hyped-up investment trend, you're not planning; you're reacting. And by the time you hear about that big winner stock or "next big thing," it's too late. The market has already moved.

This kind of FOMO-driven behavior has consequences. You may have heard Apple or Google has doubled in value, and now you want in. But if those stocks weren't in your portfolio from the beginning, the issue isn't that you need to change your portfolio. The issue is that you built that portfolio to ignore those kinds of stocks in the first place. Worse, if you're the one managing your investments and constantly second-guessing yourself, maybe you shouldn't be managing your assets at all. Investing without a plan or advisor is less like wealth building and more like gambling.

Most people aren't investors. They're speculators. Their entire strategy is built on hope and prayer instead of real economic planning. They follow online financial gurus who throw around technical jargon like "candlestick patterns" or "momentum signals," as if that somehow equates to actual planning. Those charts, forecasts, and candles? They're not real strategies. They're guesses. And many of those guesses are about as sound as throwing chicken bones in a pile and attempting to read the future from them. You aren't going to have anything solid to lean on, because guesses like these aren't based on reality.

Just look at how the big financial institutions play the game. Every year, JP Morgan, Goldman Sachs, and Merrill Lynch release market forecasts: "We expect a 5% return from U.S. equities this year." How do they get that number? Simple. If the market averaged 15% over the last five years and the historical average is 10%, they assume it'll slow down to 5% to "revert to the mean." That's not insight. That's arithmetic dressed up as prophecy.

Markets are volatile. Always have been. Always will be. You can't time them correctly. Nobody predicted when the Dow would jump nearly 3,000 points in a single day because the government paused tariffs. Nobody could explain why it dropped 1,000 points the next day. Nothing fundamentally changed in twenty-four hours, but prices did. That's why your financial plan *can't* hinge on daily market swings.

Instead, focus on what *can* be controlled. I tell clients: there are two things I can guarantee. One, we can help get you protected from the financial bad things that happen in life. Second, we can help you save and invest 20% of your income. You should have a *reasonable* target rate of return that you are trying to achieve. Everything else? That's up to the markets. They'll do what they do, and over long periods, yes, they generally go up. But you must be prepared for the stretches where they don't. Beating a benchmark or even matching it doesn't really matter with a real strategy.

Also, stop letting politics dictate your investment decisions. Markets have gone up regardless of the party in control. Your money doesn't care who you voted for. The only surefire strategy is to keep buying and keep holding, as long as you don't need that money in the next year or two. If you do? It shouldn't be in the market in the first place.

So, resist the urge to adjust your sails constantly. Your financial ship is better off with a steady hand and a long-term course. The winds will change. But that doesn't mean you should. Trust your plan. Stick to it. And stop overcorrecting every time someone posts a hot take on Twitter.

IS THERE SUCH A THING AS THE PERFECT FINANCIAL PLAN?

Life is never perfect. And when it comes to finances, perfection can indeed be the enemy of the good. Personally, I don't believe in perfection. I believe in optimal.

Perfection implies a static, unchanging end state, as if you can just plug in the correct numbers, check all the boxes, and coast through life unscathed. That's not how this works. Life is messy. Markets move. Kids get sick. Furnaces break. Job offers change. Emotions flare up. The best financial plan is the one that's adaptable enough to weather all that and simple enough that you don't unravel the whole thing every time a headline spooks you.

For the people who constantly tinker, those who can't help but check the market five times a day or who make decisions based on what cable news or Reddit said yesterday, take a breath. Seriously. If you've built a plan that accounts for your short-term needs, mid-term goals, and long-term dreams, then sit tight. Constantly tweaking your plan because of fear or FOMO usually does more harm than good. The moment you see a market swing, it's already too late to react. You're chasing yesterday's news with today's money.

Now, don't get me wrong. If you're the kind of person who loves digging into spreadsheets and plotting out your trajectory, I get it. I love a good Excel spreadsheet. But even tinkerers need a Yoda, someone to challenge their assumptions and hold them back from, say, selling their investments to buy a $104,000 Mercedes after taking a $30,000 pay cut. (Yes, that really happened.)

Most people cannot do it on their own. However, most people also think that financial planning is only about numbers and spreadsheets. It's not. A real financial planner doesn't just run your numbers. They talk you off the ledge. They keep you from buying depreciating assets with delusional confidence. They remind you that intelligent people still make dumb choices when emotion gets in the driver's seat. And sometimes—honestly, often—that's the most valuable service we provide.

I've met young professionals making six figures who, on paper, should be thriving, but they're drowning. I've also met seventy-year-old physicians who cannot stop making rounds, and still don't have enough money to meet their needs. Not because they don't earn enough, but because they torpedo their financial future with lifestyle inflation, bad habits, and a profound misunderstanding of what wealth is or any idea about what the American dream should be. Because of our Instagram-heavy lifestyle, where many of us spend hours scrolling through posts and videos of users showcasing what they have, one could easily believe that success is based on how much you have and how much you spend.

So, does a perfect plan exist? No.

But a well-built, thoughtfully managed, behavior-aware plan does. One that works with who you are, not who Instagram tells you to be. And when life throws you a curveball, that's the plan that keeps you from panic selling your future for a flashy present.

Yes, if you're wondering: the course can always be changed. But only if you want it to change. That's the most challenging part, changing your behavior.

WHY YOU NEED TO CHANGE YOUR CONSUMER DRIVEN BEHAVIOR

Kids these days. They are constantly asking us for the new thing, whether that's a new phone, a new gadget, a new video game, tickets to a very expensive Taylor Swift concert, or trendy new clothes that will just fall apart in a few weeks. If you have children, you know the pull of the consumer culture is very ,strong. But it doesn't just affect the young people. It affects everyone who exists in this world.

There's something deeply embedded in our culture, this unspoken checklist that defines what it means to be "successful." Buy a house. Drive two (or three) cars. Have the newest iPhone, the slickest tablet, the freshly remodeled kitchen with quartz counters and mosaic walls. These have become the *earmarks of success*, the visible signals that you've "made it." But here's the thing: having the stuff doesn't mean you've earned the lifestyle. Somewhere along the way, consumer culture replaced common sense, and suddenly people felt *entitled* to what used to be the rewards of hard work. It's not about who's built something sustainable. It's about who can flex it first on Instagram.

Now, don't get me wrong, there are absolutely people who *have* earned the right to enjoy luxury. They worked their butts off. They sacrificed. They saved and planned. They deserve a nice vacation or an upgraded car because they did it the right way.

But there's also a growing crowd of folks who think they *deserve* those things just because they've seen others with them. I see this all the time with younger generations, as well as within family-run businesses. The first generation starts a business from nothing, working ninety-hour weeks, skipping family dinners, grinding every day. The second generation saw the sacrifice, respected it, and continued to build. But by the time the third generation rolls around, they only see the *results*: the house, the cars, the lifestyle. They didn't see the blood, sweat, and ramen noodles it took to get there.

You don't have to come from a family business to fall into this trap. I see it in everyday clients. One generation hustled. The next got comfortable. The third? Entitled. They weren't told "no" enough. They didn't have to struggle or stretch. And now, they're trying to finance a $700,000 lifestyle on a $70,000 salary, and wondering why they feel constantly behind.

The problem is that we've gone from being a society that *makes* things to one that just *buys* things. Need groceries? Have them delivered in an hour. Want new shoes? Click, tap, done. That convenience has its perks, but it's killing our ability to delay gratification. Technology has trained us to expect immediate results and effortless upgrades. But real wealth? That takes time. It takes effort. It takes patience—and a lot of "no's" along the way.

Consumer culture turns everything into a transaction. But financial stability isn't transactional. It's *behavioral*. And unless you've been told "no" by life a few times, you'll struggle to find the drive it takes to build a lasting financial foundation. I know this sounds harsh, but sometimes I feel more like a sponsor at a financial AA meeting than a planner. Because yes, entitlement can be an addiction too, one that keeps people from building real wealth. It's the addiction to appearing successful instead of *being* financially stable.

So if you find yourself wondering why your six-figure salary doesn't feel like enough, or why you're still stressed despite your "stuff," take a step back, ask yourself: "What am I trying to prove?" Because chances are, the only person keeping you stuck is you, and the myth you've been sold about what success *should* look like.

CHAPTER 7

THE PSYCHOLOGY BEHIND OUR FINANCIAL DECISIONS

Generic financial advice sounds good on paper: Max out your 401(k). Open a Roth. Do a backdoor Roth. Pay off your mortgage. Don't pay off your mortgage. Buy the dip. Never sell. Fire your financial advisor and do it yourself. Invest in this stock. Don't invest in that stock. Stop spending. Spend more. Are you exhausted yet? It's no wonder most people feel overwhelmed. The problem isn't just the advice. It's also the assumptions built into it. There are many.

Take, for instance, the idea that you need to check your portfolio often or make financial adjustments every time the market hiccups. That kind of reactive behavior may feel productive, but it actually erodes the foundation of a genuine financial plan. And just to clarify, your *portfolio* is not your *plan*. A portfolio is just one component of a broader, more holistic approach. When you treat your investments like a day trading sandbox, bouncing in and out of Apple or Robinhood stocks based on what Jim Cramer screamed yesterday, you're not building wealth. You're chasing dopamine.

And while we're talking about misconceptions, let's address one of the most emotionally charged: providing for adult children. I saw a stat recently that half of parents with Gen Z or Millennial children are spending an average of $1,500 a month (nearly $18,000 a year) to financially support their grown kids. These are kids who, by all logic, should be earning their own income and learning how to manage their own expenses. But instead, we've normalized this quiet transfer of wealth in the wrong direction. Not only is it potentially wrecking the retirement plans of those parents, but it also sets up a cycle of dependency that's hard to break. One day, those same kids may have to support *you*, because you spent your golden years floating their lifestyle.

I've worked with high-income earners (doctors, attorneys, business owners) who are told to follow the same script: max out retirement accounts first, then invest anything left. But what about student loans? What about mortgages, car payments, and emergencies? What about *liquidity*? That part often gets ignored. Yet without a cushion to help you sleep at night, all that compounding wealth doesn't mean much. A great plan isn't about chasing maximum return. It's about designing something that works when life throws curveballs. Trust me. Life *will* throw curveballs. That's why your plan should be flexible, not fickle. There's a big difference.

So what should you do? Set up your plan. Automate it. Disengage. Focus on your life, your family, and your work.

A good financial plan is like a strong immune system: if it's working well, you shouldn't even notice it. The rest? Noise. The financial media industry *wants* you to be anxious. They want you afraid, reactive, and convinced that one more click, one more tweak, one more subscription will save you from financial ruin. But at the end of every segment, do you ever actually feel better? Probably not.

THE 'EXPERTS' CAN'T HELP YOU

When's the last time you watched a segment on Bloomberg, CNBC, or heard a rant from Dave Ramsey or Suze Orman and walked away feeling calm, reassured, and financially empowered? It rarely happens. That's because their model only works if you stay scared. If you're not afraid, if you're not convinced the sky is falling or that you're making catastrophic mistakes, then you stop tuning in. And if you stop tuning in, they stop selling ads, books, and subscriptions. They lose revenue, eyeballs, and prestige. All of these losses are a death sentence for any media outlet.

These outlets are not incentivized to help you manage your money better. They're incentivized to stir conflict and promote contradictory ideas, just to keep the conversation going and the clicks coming. They want to get better ratings and keep their brand going. It's like being the editor of *Forbes* and deciding whether your job is to publish *the answer*, or to fill pages with the same recycled ideas rebranded each month for maximum circulation. Often, it's the latter. Articles contradict themselves from one issue to the next, not because there's new insight, but because confusion sells.

Even if it's not outright sinister, it's still misleading. Many of these experts don't even *have* the answers. They want you to lean on them, trust them, subscribe to their worldview—but it's mostly guesswork dressed up as authority. And buried deep in every investment perspective, you'll find the same line: *"Past results are not indicative of future performance."* So, what are we even reading for? For the average person, much of it's just noise, especially when it's not tied to a personalized plan.

Nowhere is this disconnect more evident than in the debate over so-called "exclusive" investment opportunities. I've read comments online where people are outraged that certain private equity or private credit opportunities are only open to accredited investors, meaning you need to have a high income or a high net worth even to qualify.

The public outcry is always the same: *"The rich get richer! Why are we being left out?"* But here's the truth: those restrictions exist to protect people from making huge mistakes. Those investments are *illiquid.* They're riskier. And they're not built for people who might panic and demand their money back next week. That kind of instability doesn't just hurt the investor—it hurts the entire system.

If you want a better metaphor for what your financial life *should* feel like, think about data centers. Picture your personal financial plan as a secure server locked away in a climate-controlled room, with a security guard checking in occasionally to ensure everything is running smoothly. That's what your finances should feel like: calm, guarded, and mostly hands off. You don't need to rip open the box every night to see if it's still working.

This is where automation becomes your greatest ally. It's one of the reasons employer-sponsored retirement plans are so effective.

Once you sign up and commit to contributing 3%, 4%, or 5% of your paycheck, the work is done. You don't have to think about it. You don't have to log in every two weeks and manually transfer money. If most people had to make those decisions manually every payday, they simply wouldn't. Not even once.

Automation *is* accountability. It builds consistency. It turns intention into habit. And it frees up your energy to live the rest of your life.

So if all these financial influencers, talking heads, and headline chasers make you feel like you're always behind, that you're never doing enough, that's precisely what they want. But you don't have to play that game.

Ask yourself just two questions:

1. Are you fully protected from the bad things that can happen in life?
2. Are you saving 15–20% of your income?

WHAT YOU NEED TO KNOW ABOUT INVESTMENTS BEFORE YOU START INVESTING

If there's one real-world financial lesson I wish every client understood from day one, it's this: the amount of money you save is far more important than the rate of return you get on your investments. Savings *consistently* outperform returns. That may not sound sexy, but it's the truth.

So why do people get so caught up in chasing returns? Why are so many of us glued to headlines or obsessing over following hot stock? It's because flashy investments make great stories. The home run swings are what get talked about at backyard barbecues and on financial talk shows. It's the movies. The bragging rights. "My friend doubled his money in XYZ stock." Sounds amazing, right? But when I ask, "How much did he invest?" most people don't know. Maybe it was $1,000. So now he has $2,000. Incredible story, but in the big picture of financial freedom, who cares!

And here's where it gets even trickier: the average rate of return is one of the most misleading metrics in investing. Let me break that down.

Average Return vs. Actual Result

+100%   **-50%**   Average annual return:
25%
(Arithmetic average)

START	Year 2	Year 2	
$100,000	**$200,000**	**$100,000**	Actual return:
$100,000	$200,000	$100,000	**0%** (Before taxes & fees)

$100,000 → **$200,000**

Say I create a private investment opportunity and promise you a 25% average annual return. I show you exactly what the return will be each year, and I even register it with the SEC. Sounds incredible, right? Here's how it plays out:

► **YEAR 1:** You earn a 100% return on your $100,000. Now you've got $200,000.

► **YEAR 2:** You lose 50%. Now you're back to $100,000.

The *average* rate of return is 25%, but your actual return is zero, and that's before taxes and fees. You *lost* money even though the marketing pitch says you gained. It's the financial equivalent of a magic trick. And this kind of math is baked into several mutual funds, several stock projections, and several investment calculators you'll find online.

So why doesn't anyone talk about this? "I invested consistently for twenty years and built long-term wealth through discipline" doesn't make for exciting blog content. But that's the real story behind financial success.

Let's take this further. I've shown this scenario in real time with clients:

Imagine someone starts with nothing at age twenty-two and invests $20,000 every year for forty-three years, until they retire at sixty-five. Assuming a textbook 10% return from the S&P 500, they should theoretically have around $13 million. But that's in a perfect world.

Real life doesn't work that way. Here's what will inevitably happen.

- ► You miss a few years.
- ► You pull money out to buy a house.
- ► You panic when the market drops and sell at a low price.
- ► You pay investment fees.
- ► You pay taxes.
- ► Children need education that requires a massive tuition check.
- ► Your car breaks down.
- ► You get sick or injured.
- ► A loved one needs help.
- ► Your water heater breaks.

After accounting for all of that, your $13 million might turn into $5 million. And yes, $5 million is still a lot of money, but let's be clear: you just lost $8 million of what *could have been*. That's a massive opportunity cost. It's the cost of not understanding the complete picture of investing.

But let's be fair: people don't fail because they're bad at math. Almost everyone I walk through this with *gets it*. The real problem is that no one ever took the time to show them how the math of money works, and how it's *not* the same thing as math on paper. You and I walk into a room, and I place three fresh oranges on the table. Tomorrow, I'll come back and put down three more. That's six oranges now. But if we walk away and return 20 years later, those six oranges won't be there. They'll be dust. Rotted. Ants and mold will have done their job.

Purchasing Power Decays Over Time

20 years

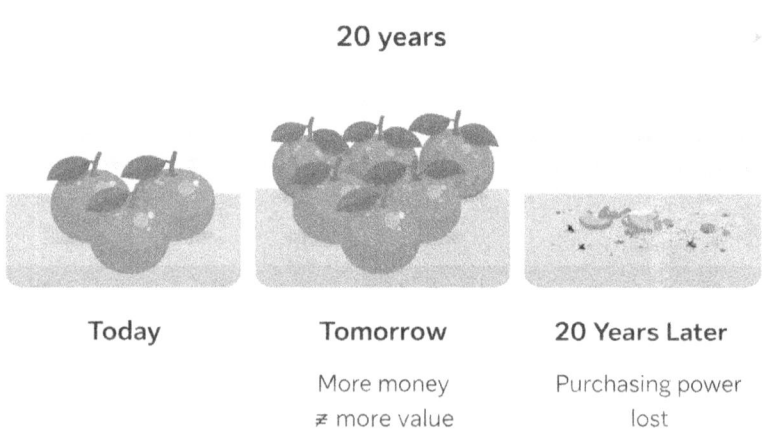

Today	Tomorrow	20 Years Later
	More money	Purchasing power
	≠ more value	lost

That's inflation. Over time, your money loses purchasing power, just like those oranges lose their substance. That's why it's not enough just to save. You must save consistently and invest in a way that outpaces inflation while avoiding unnecessary losses from fees, taxes, or poor timing.

And this is where people fall short, not because they're lazy or stupid, but because we live in a world that promises results without habits. They hear that all they have to do is "buy the S&P 500 and hold." Sounds easy. But in reality, *nobody lives a perfect financial life*. Nobody invests exactly $20,000 every single year without fail. Nobody avoids every emotional mistake. Nobody escapes taxes and fees.

This is why the greatest lie in investing is that it's about picking the right stock or beating the market. The real truth? It's about doing the right thing over and over and over again, even when it's boring, especially when it's boring.

Yes, investments matter. However, it's more how much you contribute, how often you contribute, and how consistent you are over the decades—that's what builds wealth. A real financial plan has a target rate of return that you are trying to achieve, not just shooting for the stars. So forget the home runs. Ignore the headlines. Stop chasing "average returns." Instead, focus on what you can control: your savings rate, your timeline, and your behavior. And let the math—the real math—work in your favor.

EMOTIONS MAKE FOR BAD INVESTMENTS

If you've ever looked at your investment account and thought, *"This isn't going the way I planned,"* you're not alone. You're the norm. Most people underperform in the market, not because of bad investments, but because of bad behavior. Let me show you one of my favorite charts. Over the last twenty or so years, the average investor earned just **2.5%** annually. That's because the S&P 500, emerging markets, small caps, high-yield bonds, and REITs were doing dramatically better. So what happened? What stopped investors from earning the higher returns the market actually delivered?

COMMON INVESTOR BEHAVIOR
20-YEAR ANNUALIZED RETURNS BY ASSET CLASS (2001-2021)

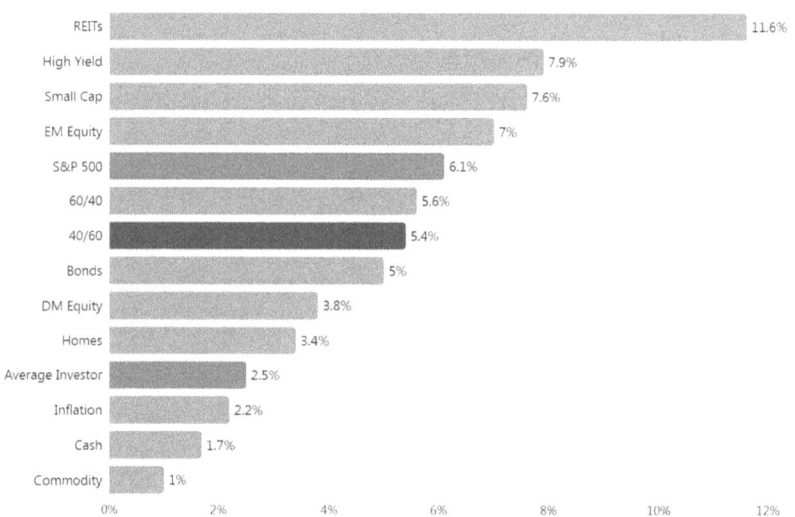

SOURCE: Barclays; Bloomberg; FactSet; Standard & Poor's; J.P. Morgan Asset Management; and (Bottom) Dalbar, Inc.; MSCI; NAREIT; and Russell. Index definitions as stated in the original figure. *Guide to the Markets*—U.S. Data are as of March 31, 2021.

Emotions.

If you had simply bought a diversified portfolio and held on, no tweaking, no panic selling, no second-guessing, you could have earned close to **6%**. But most people didn't. Most people bailed when things got hard. Most people tried to time the market. Most people let fear or overconfidence take the wheel. Let me show you what I mean. Imagine two investors. Investor A stayed the course through the 2008 financial crisis. They didn't touch their portfolio. Investor B panicked, sold during the crash, and didn't get back in until a year later. That one decision, missing just a single year, cost them $165,000.

That's the cost of emotional decision-making.

So why do people ignore good advice from their financial planners? Why do they skip insurance, skip saving, or decide that Robinhood has all the answers?

It comes down to three things:

1. **EGO:** We believe we're smarter than everyone else. We assume we're the exception.

2. **OVERCONFIDENCE:** We think, "That won't happen to me."

3. **LACK OF SAVINGS MENTALITY:** We'd rather trust our intuition than build habits.

However, if you truly want a financial plan that works, you must start with humility. You have to admit: *"I don't know everything."* That humility opens the door to working with a real professional, and trusting their advice even when it contradicts what your friends, coworkers, or TikTok are saying.

The problem gets even worse when people receive stock compensation from their employers. I see this all the time. They assume, *"Well, I work here—I know the company—I know the stock will go up."* But they almost always assume wrong. Either the stock dips, or it doesn't grow as expected, and they're left holding the bag.

Take IPOs, for example. Everyone rushes in. They buy high, excited by the hype. But twenty days later, the average IPO has dropped **66%**.[8] People panic and sell. The same people who say,

---

[8] Mackintosh, Phil. "What Happens to IPOs Over the Long Run?" *Nasdaq*, April 15, 2021.

"If only I had bought Apple in 1985 ..." conveniently forget that they would have had to **hold it for 25 years** before seeing real growth. Who's going to do that? Almost no one.

We want instant gratification. We want the GameStop miracle. But GameStop isn't a strategy, it's a casino. It could be up to $100 a share again, and I still wouldn't touch it. The fundamentals just aren't there. No one's buying video games in brick-and-mortar stores anymore. If you knew anything about the video game industry, you'd see this stock is all sizzle and no substance.

The reality is: *there's no such thing as a "safe" investment*, not in the short term. To succeed, you either need extraordinary patience ... or extraordinary forgetfulness. Seriously. Some of the biggest wins I've seen were from people who bought stock decades ago, only to forget they owned it completely. One of my favorite examples? 50 Cent. The rapper took Bitcoin payments for an album, forgot about it, and ended up sitting on a pile of digital gold.[9]

But those are outliers. Most people don't buy and forget. Most people watch. They stress. They make changes. They tinker. And they usually lose.

That's why it's not just about returns. It's about *behavior*. It's about creating a system you can stick to, one that's designed to work even when you don't feel like it. Investing isn't about knowing the market; it's about understanding it. It's about knowing *yourself*. So the next time you feel tempted to make a sudden move, ask yourself: "Am I reacting out of emotion ... or following a plan?" One of those paths leads to growth. The other leads to regret.

---

[9] Daniel Liberto, "Rapper 50 Cent Just Realized He's a Bitcoin Millionaire," *Investopedia*, June 25, 2019.

CHAPTER 8

WHO ARE YOU GOING TO CALL? FINANCIAL MYTHBUSTERS

L et's play a game. Pretend every dollar you earn has a designated location: one dollar for groceries, one dollar for rent, one dollar for that one streaming service you *swear* you canceled three months ago. At the end of the month, you've accounted for every single cent and you're sitting pretty at … zero.

That's "zero-based budgeting," and it's one of the many financial ideas floating around out there that sounds helpful in theory but feels like a full-time job in practice. I'd argue that if your budget ends at zero every month, you're doing it wrong. Designating every dollar may sound like a great way to save money, but it's not.

We're going to bust some financial myths that everyone knows about. These are the kinds of pointless maxims you hear from family members or TV personalities who might be just a little out of touch themselves. If these "truths" were working, more people would be succeeding financially, and they're not. If assigning every dollar to a task was *actually* a magic formula for wealth, wouldn't more families be thriving? Wouldn't more people be budgeting like pros and crushing debt?

You can't just stare at your spreadsheet and say, "Sorry, emergency, you weren't in the budget." Life doesn't care about your carefully itemized zero-based plan. And when you "fail" at a rigid system like that, one that was never designed to handle real human lives, you start believing you're failing financially. That belief leads people to give up. That's the real problem.

We're told by our parents, our neighbors, and our aging family dentist that if we're not following these cookie-cutter methods, budgeting every penny, snowballing every debt, or getting a magical 12% return from "any old mutual fund" (yes, that's an actual claim), then we're doing something wrong. The truth? Most of these systems overlook reality, and they certainly disregard emotion. They assume you can make financial decisions in a vacuum. They assume you'll never hit a bump, never feel overwhelmed, never need to buy a last-minute birthday present for your kid's entire class because, well, school politics.

The debt snowball is another classic. It sounds great on paper: pay off your smallest debts first, roll those payments into the next one, and so on. In practice? You end up throwing every spare dollar at your loans with no money left for life's curveballs. Then your car breaks down, or your dishwasher dies, or your AC gives out during the hottest July on record, and guess what? You're back to borrowing again. All your "progress" just got wiped out.

See, none of this advice is *entirely* wrong; it just lacks context, nuance, and flexibility. And let's be honest, some basic empathy. It's a bit puritanical and rigid and does not account for people who have kids, health problems, complex living situations,

YOUR PLAN *HAS* TO WORK EVEN WHEN LIFE DOESN'T.

Ready to debunk some nonsense? Let's go myth busting.

MYTH NUMBER ONE

MAX OUT YOUR RETIREMENT ACCOUNT

Let's talk about a myth that's been pounded into people's heads so relentlessly that it's practically gospel: "You have to max out your 401(k) or IRA. Immediately. No questions asked. That's the only way to retire comfortably." It's the classic line from every talking head and financial personality: *Live below your means. Redirect your coffee budget into your retirement plan. Sacrifice everything now so maybe, if all goes well, you can enjoy life at sixty.*

I'm not against contributing to your retirement plan. Far from it. If your employer offers a 401(k) contribution match, you should take advantage of it. That's just smart. Some employers are even allowing matches to help pay down student loans, which is a significant win. However, maxing out your retirement accounts when you're still twenty-five, thirty, or even thirty-five? That should not be the first step in your financial life. It should typically be one of the last.

Why? Because those accounts are illiquid, which is a fancy way of saying you can't touch that money. A traditional 401(k)? You're not getting to that until you're fifty-nine and a half. A Roth IRA? Yes, you can access your contributions after five years, but too much can happen in that time. So much more can happen in the thirty or forty years between now and when you're finally allowed to enjoy that money without penalty. You might get married. You might get divorced! You might have to have a very expensive lifesaving surgery. Your house might burn down. There are far too many variables, and because these situations are relatively common (we all age, we all get sick, we all fall in and out of love), you will experience an event where that money could be better spent.

Yes, it's true: there are more 401(k) millionaires now than ever before. And I love that. That's progress. But here's what no one says out loud: "What good is being a millionaire at sixty if you lived like a monk for thirty years to get there?" By the time you are old enough to retire, you will hurt all over. Your body will not want to travel or try new things unless you are in incredible shape. You will not be able to see as well, you will not be able to eat as much, and you certainly won't be able to do everything you want to do, because of the limitations that naturally come with age.

What good is retiring with $2 million if you skipped every family vacation, never went to Disney with your kids, drove a car you hated, and lived every day with a calculator in your hand, trying to figure out how to afford a movie night?

You are allowed to enjoy your life now. Financial planning is not a punishment. It's a framework to help you live better, not to delay joy indefinitely. You don't have to stop saving—that's not what I'm advocating. You should still save and avoid reckless spending. You shouldn't keep up with the Joneses. But you also shouldn't be living alone in a hut in Tibet, living only off bread and water. It is all about balance. You're only given one life, so don't destroy it either way.

You shouldn't have to choose between maxing out your 401(k) and making memories while your kids are still little. You shouldn't be guilted into thinking that skipping a latte today is going to magically buy you a yacht tomorrow. Build flexibility. Build liquidity. Build joy. That's a better financial plan. Because your life isn't lived in the future, it's lived right now.

MYTH NUMBER TWO

AVOID DEBT AT ALL COSTS

Most people born before 2005 have heard the adage: *"Avoid credit cards. Never carry debt. Use debit for everything. Live within your means. Better yet, live below them."* You've probably heard it a hundred times from the financial guru crowd. Here's the problem though. This piece of advice really does not make sense when paired with another popular statement. You've probably heard it shouted into a microphone by some guy on Instagram standing in front of a rented Lamborghini: *"Buy assets, not liabilities! Invest in real estate! Build a business! Stocks! Passive income!"*

Okay. But ... with *what?* Unless you're a millionaire or inherited a massive sum of cash, you probably don't have the kinds of resources you would need to buy those assets.

"Go buy a business," they say. Sure. Just open up that secret suitcase of spare millions you've been hiding under the bed. "Acquire real estate," they cheer. Awesome! Just grab your monocle, stroll into a bank, and ask for a cool $500K mortgage on your lunch break. Careful, though, you might pass Go and collect $200, or you might end up on Park Place and have to pay rent. And then you've lost the Monopoly game.

To acquire the so-called "assets" these gurus keep hyping, you almost always have to take on debt first. Buying a rental property usually means a mortgage. Starting a business might mean a loan, a line of credit, or draining your savings. And guess what? That debt is a *liability*. But wait, isn't the whole point to *avoid* liabilities? See the issue?

Let me be clear: carrying high interest debt in the long term isn't smart. That's just math. But the idea that the solution is only to use debit cards and treat all debt like it's financial arsenic? That's kind of dumb.

Credit, when used correctly, is a tool, not a trap. Avoiding it altogether doesn't make you disciplined. It makes you un-prepared. Building credit is essential if you want to rent an apartment, buy a home, lease a car, or even open a business someday. If your financial strategy is based on fear rather than functionality, you're not planning; you're hiding.

The same black-and-white thinking also applies to Roth IRAs. You'll hear, "Roth, Roth, Roth!" like it's the answer to every tax problem. And yes, Roth IRAs and Roth 401(k)s are great options if you want tax-free growth and distributions in retirement. That's useful. But guess what? You don't need to choose just one. You don't need to pick Roth *or* traditional. You can do both. A real financial strategy *includes* both, because future tax rates are unpredictable, and the best thing you can do is build flexibility into your plan.

Most people are unaware that in retirement, you're only taxed on the amount you withdraw from a traditional IRA or 401(k) account. If you're in a lower tax bracket when you retire, which many people are, then it could make more sense to defer taxes now rather than pay them upfront with a Roth. And if you're in a high tax bracket now and stuffing every dollar into Roths? You might be giving Uncle Sam more than necessary.

There are even *other* vehicles beyond Roths and 401(k)s. Think municipal bonds. Think whole life insurance with cash value. Whole life insurance isn't evil. It's not a scam. It's a financial tool. You can buy whole life insurance **and** invest. You can hold traditional **and** Roth accounts. The comparison of products is crazy, because often the answer is having both. You can use debt responsibly. You can have a credit card without maxing it out on sneakers and concert tickets.

This isn't about choosing one path. It's about creating a plan that adapts to your life, goals, and future. Don't fall for the myth that it's all-or-nothing, black-or-white, Roth-or-bust. The financial world is not as simple as that. And you're smarter than that.

MYTH NUMBER THREE

PASSIVE INCOME WILL SET YOU FREE

Time to burst an oversized, shiny bubble. *There's no such thing as passive income.*

If I had a dollar for every time someone told me they were

working on their "passive income stream," I'd have … well, *actual* income, which is more than I can say for most people chasing that dream.

Look, I get the appeal. Who doesn't want to sip something cold on a beach while their money just multiplies in the background? You've probably seen it in a YouTube ad: some guy standing in front of a rented mansion claiming he makes six figures while doing *nothing*. He owns real estate. He has an e-commerce store. He's "made it."

Here's what they don't tell you: all of those so-called "passive" income streams are built on a foundation of very active effort, stress, and usually debt. Real estate doesn't just sit there generating money like a magical goose laying golden eggs. That tenant? They're going to call you at 2:00 a.m. when the toilet breaks. They might skip rent. They might trash the place. Now, you need a property manager, which eats into your cash flow, and it's going to take longer to pay off your mortgage and make a return.

Even celebrity-level investing isn't immune. Celebrities with seemingly infinite amounts of cash invest heavily in buying British soccer clubs, small islands, restaurant chains, or social media websites. They never start collecting on that investment right away. It's a losing battle, even for someone with Oscar winning actor money. You aren't going to figure it out right away.

So what about "passive" stock income? If you purchased Apple stock in 1985 and forgot about it for thirty years, *maybe you'll see something*. But that's the key: you would have had to forget about it. The average investor can't sit on a stock for a decade without checking their portfolio seventeen times a week. In fact, most people sell as soon as the market dips. That's why, despite all the impressive long-term returns of the S&P 500, the average investor does not earn as much as they could, not because the market failed, but because they misbehaved.

Passive income? It's generally a fairy tale. *The only people truly making money off passive income are the ones selling you the idea of passive income.*

So, stop chasing "easy money." It doesn't exist. Wealth requires effort, either up front or continuously, but always more than a weekend webinar and a Pinterest board of investment quotes. Don't let a one line catchphrase shape your entire financial mindset. Building wealth isn't about reciting catchy slogans; it's about creating a strategy that works in the real world.

MYTH NUMBER FOUR

IF YOU FOLLOW THE PATH OF THE GREAT FINANCIAL GURUS, YOU'LL BE RICH

One of the most repeated pieces of advice in the finance world is, "Well, Warren Buffett says just to buy index funds." Great. That's not bad advice for the average person. The problem? That's not actually what Warren Buffett *does.* Pull up the Berkshire Hathaway portfolio, the company Buffett runs, and guess how many index funds or Exchange Traded Funds (ETFs) you'll find? *Zero.* None. Berkshire Hathaway doesn't buy index funds. It buys *businesses.* And it doesn't buy fifty shares at a time on Robinhood, either.

Buffett's moves aren't casual or comparable to your monthly contribution into a 401(k). He writes checks for hundreds of millions of dollars at a time to take controlling stakes in companies. He's not just investing; he's acquiring ownership, board seats, and power. His investment strategy is less "set it and forget it" and more "CEO whisperer with $300 billion in cash."

People love to talk about how much cash Buffett is sitting on. "Oh, he must know something's coming!" No, he's just waiting to make his next mega acquisition. When your portfolio is the size of a small country's GDP, you don't "buy the dip," you buy the company.

And yet, here we are with apps that let you "mirror" celebrity investors. Want to copy Warren Buffett's portfolio? Guess what? You already can. It's called buying a share of Berkshire Hathaway. That's the vehicle. That's where his money is. There's no secret side account where he's day trading Dogecoin on his lunch break.

Even if you manage to mimic his investments through some app, you're still late to the party. By the time Buffett's move is made public, the stock's price has already jumped 8–10%, just from the news that he bought it. So when you buy in, you're paying a premium. He got in when it was cheap. You're buying it hyped-up and overpriced. That's not investing; that's chasing.

The same phenomenon happens with index funds like the S&P 500. When the committee announces a new stock has been added to the index, that stock jumps 8–10%, *just because it was added.* People pour into the fund, buying high without understanding why. And when companies get kicked off the index? Their prices drop. Ironically, that's when you should consider buying them, after the overreaction.

This is the same pattern over and over again: reactive investing masquerading as strategy. You're not getting the inside scoop. You're reading the press release after the whales have already eaten. So no, you can't just follow the big names in finance and expect the same outcome. You're not playing the same game. Warren Buffett doesn't need liquidity. You do. He doesn't need to plan for daycare, new tires, or a trip to Disney before his kid turns ten. He is not your model.

If you really admire Buffett, take the part of his advice that *is* relevant: be patient, invest consistently, and focus on the long term. But stop treating every quote like it's a golden ticket. Because if Warren Buffett's moves worked for the average investor, he wouldn't be Warren Buffett anymore.

CHAPTER 9

HOW TO HELP SET YOUR KIDS UP FOR SUCCESS

When it comes to financial planning, one of the most universal goals I hear from my clients is that they want their kids to succeed. Usually this means they want to give them some kind of generational wealth, pay for their college tuition, help them find a good career path, or have insurance in case the worst happens.

But here's the problem: most parents are following outdated or product-driven advice that doesn't actually equip their kids with what they need. They're told to "get a 529 savings plan" without any broader context or understanding of *why* or *how* those tools fit into a strategy. The industry is leading with products instead of solutions. So I challenge you to flip that approach on its head, whether you have kids or are planning to have kids. The right question to ask is: *"What kind of financial foundation can I build for my child, and how can I model healthy financial behavior?"*

Here are some statements that I have said before in this book, but they bear repeating.

PROTECT YOUR KIDS

One of the earliest, and often most overlooked, ways to help set children up for financial success is making sure *you're protected*. That means having life insurance, disability coverage, and emergency savings in place. Why? Because if something happens to you and your family isn't protected, it won't matter what kind of college savings account you opened; your child's future will be at risk.

It may not sound like it's "for your kids," but it is. Your protection is the first building block in their financial future.

DON'T DUMP EVERYTHING INTO A COLLEGE FUND

Many parents rush into college savings plans while still paying off debt or living paycheck to paycheck. Yeah, you're right, college is incredibly expensive, but by the time your child is of age, it will be even more expensive (unless the world ends before then). If you're directing hundreds of dollars to a savings account but are taking out loans or maxing out credit cards, then you're on shaky ground.

Instead, focus on freeing up cash flow first: reduce debts, lower taxes, and build a solid emergency fund. When you have breathing room, then you can begin to consistently save for your child's future without sacrificing your present stability.

TALK ABOUT MONEY EARLY AND OFTEN

Financial literacy starts at home, not in a classroom. Teaching kids about money should be ongoing, not a onetime conversation. Let them see how you manage savings, talk openly about spending, and involve them in real decisions, like choosing between eating out or saving for a family vacation.

Yes, money is a stressful conversation starter, but it really doesn't have to be. Stop making money a taboo topic. The more normal and open the conversation, the more confident and capable your children will be later in life.

Perhaps the most important message for parents: don't let shame about your financial journey hold you back from teaching your kids. Many people feel wary or unworthy about financial advice because they don't have a certain income or investment portfolio. But *having a plan*, even with modest income, puts you ahead of most. Let your kids learn from your mistakes. Make sure they don't repeat them once they hit adulthood.

If you model financial intention and structure, your kids will learn that it's not about having the most money; it's about making the most of what you have. That mindset is a gift that compounds across generations.

IT'S NOT ALL ABOUT COLLEGE

While college is a common milestone, it's not the only one. A financially secure child may someday need help with a first home, launching a business, or covering healthcare expenses. I encourage families to plan with flexibility, not just for one predetermined goal. That could mean building a family trust, creating a multiuse savings account, or simply having open conversations about expectations.

MAKE THE HEAD START COUNT FOR SOMETHING

You have children, and they're getting older. You want them to succeed and to learn about how the world works. The best places to start are with the basics: open a bank account, automate savings, and help with benefits in their first job. Don't ignore the benefits simply because they are covered under your health insurance until they are twenty-six. Get started sooner so that the transition doesn't take them by surprise.

One of the most instinctive things as a parent is to *help*. You see your kid struggling, or just starting, and you want to make life easier. Maybe you didn't get that kind of support growing up, and now that you're in a better place financially, you want to give them everything you didn't have. But don't just bail out your kids when they are struggling. You can do that, but remember that your money only goes so far. You aren't a separate bank account for your kids: you have your own goals and your dreams that you need to achieve.

On the map of life, they are at the beginning. Start simple. Take your teen or college age kid to the bank. Open up a checking account where they can learn how to pay bills and track their spending. Pair it with a savings account, and teach them how to separate spending money from sleep-well-at-night money. Show them what it means to account for all bills and upcoming transactions so they do not get confused. So what if they only make minimum wage at McDonald's? It's not about the dollar amount; it's about building the habit early. Let them make small mistakes while the stakes are low.

Another one of the best gifts you can give a young adult is *margin*—a little breathing room. If you've got the means, offer to match their savings up to a certain amount, or drop $1,000 in a separate emergency account to get them started, but only after your goals are covered and you've invested enough for your own future.

But here's the key: *don't make it a blank check*. This isn't "call mom and dad whenever you're short." This is "*I believe in giving you a foundation, but it's up to you to maintain it.*"

Teach them how to automate their savings. Even if it's $50 a month, getting used to money flowing into a savings account without thinking about it is one of the most powerful habits you can install. Show them that budget apps won't work just by paying for the app itself and forgetting to do all the rest.

Explain that this is how *real* adults build wealth, not by budgeting every new pair of Jordans, but by putting systems in place that make the future first, and let the spending come second.

Find some time to sit down with your kid after they get their first job to go over the benefits that their job might offer. Most parents don't understand these benefits themselves, so maybe the best way to set them up for success is by sending your kids to your own financial planner to discuss what makes sense for them. Most young people enter the workforce with no clue how to evaluate health insurance, retirement plans, or employer benefits. They just pick whatever is cheapest, or worse, they ignore it altogether. Many kids will assume that *you* will cover the costs of living, medical care, or other expenses.

Sit down with them. Go through their offer letter. Help them understand:

▶ What a 401(k) match is and why they should contribute enough to get it.

▶ The difference between an FSA and an HSA.

▶ Why life and disability insurance *through work* might not be enough.

▶ Transportation benefits and accidental death insurance that might not be worth it.

If you don't know those things yourself, use it as a learning opportunity. Get curious together. This stuff is confusing, but it's also critical.

AVOID COSIGNING LOANS OR CREDIT CARDS

This one might sting a bit, but hear me out: don't cosign student loans or credit cards unless you're prepared to take over the payments.

When you cosign, you're not just "helping them qualify," you're legally on the hook. And worse, you're sending a subtle signal that says, "I'll step in if this doesn't work out." This makes your teenage or young adult children think that you've got this, that you'll take care of everything, and all they have to do is relax. Even if you are paying their college tuition, making them go through the loan process can be valuable on its own. You don't want them to think you're their bank account.

That's not financial independence. That's just outsourcing

responsibility. Instead, help them understand the full cost of borrowing, show them how interest works, and encourage them to find ways to minimize debt, whether that means community college, scholarships, or working part-time.

TRANSFORM BAD ADVICE INTO A TEACHABLE MOMENT

Every single person older than the age of thirteen is on some form of social media. There's never been more financial advice out there, and never less accountability for where it leads. Between social media grifters, paid influencers, and well-meaning advice from friends and relatives, it's no wonder people are overwhelmed and confused. That includes your kids.

So instead of shielding them from the noise, teach them how to navigate it. The moment someone in your family says something like, *"You'll be in a lower tax bracket when you retire,"* or *"Buy a house as soon as you can because renting is throwing money away,"* don't let it slide. These are opportunities. Stop and ask:

- ► "Does that really make sense?"
- ► "Who benefits if we believe this?"
- ► "What would happen if we followed that advice?"
- ► "What's missing from this perspective?"

You're not being a contrarian, you're modeling critical thinking. Financial literacy doesn't come from memorizing the "rules." It comes from learning how to question the rules and where to look when the answers aren't clear.

If you're unsure how to approach the advice or need help debunking it, consider getting your financial advisor involved. Sometimes the best lesson you can teach your kid is that you don't know everything either. If a piece of advice comes up that *you're* not sure about, say so. Look it up together. Check with a reliable source. Call your financial advisor. Compare different opinions.

That does two things:

1. It teaches humility.
2. It shows them where to turn when they have questions of their own.

It also reinforces a powerful truth: *No one should be making long-term financial decisions based solely on soundbites.*

ABOUT THE AUTHOR

Ryan M. Coulter, CFP®, CLTC®, RICP®, is a financial advisor with Luttner Financial Group, a Lifetime Financial Growth Company. He has built his career helping high-income earners, business owners, healthcare professionals, and families make sense of their money in a world where traditional advice often falls short. Drawing on years of experience in financial planning—including insurance and protection design, wealth management, retirement income strategies, and small business planning—Ryan brings clarity to the complexity of modern financial life.

In his debut book, he challenges outdated "rules of thumb" and offers readers a practical, real-world framework for building a plan that fits their actual lives, not just a spreadsheet. His straightforward approach is shaped by his work with clients across the country and his conviction that good planning is not about products, but about confidence.

Ryan holds the FINRA Series 6, 7, 63, and 65 securities registrations, as well as state insurance licenses. He is a CERTIFIED FINANCIAL PLANNER™ professional, a Retirement Income Certified Professional®, and a Certified in Long-Term Care® specialist. A graduate of Pennsylvania State University with a degree in kinesiology, Ryan is passionate about education, clear communication, and helping people make informed decisions about their future.

When he's not working with clients or writing, Ryan enjoys spending time with his family and rescue dog, as well as golfing and boating. This book reflects his belief that financial planning should empower, not overwhelm, and that everyone deserves the confidence to live fully while preparing wisely for what's ahead.